Period Style

Period Style

JUDITH & MARTIN MILLER

PHOTOGRAPHY BY JAMES MERRELL

CHIEF CONTRIBUTOR: FREDA PARKER

MITCHELL BEAZLEY

PERIOD STYLE
Judith and Martin Miller
Photography by James Merrell
Chief Contributor: Freda Parker

First published in Great Britain in 1989
by Mitchell Beazley
an imprint of Reed Consumer Books Limited
Michelin House, 81 Fulham Road, London SW3 6RB
and Auckland

Senior Executive Art Editor **Jacqui Small**
Editor **Alex Towle**
Assistant Art Editor **Larraine Lacey**
Editorial Assistants **Jaspal Kharay**
Design Assistant **Camilla Joerin**
Production **Ted Timberlake**

Reprinted 1990
First paperback edition 1993

Revised edition published in 1998

Contributor **John Wainwright**
Executive Editor **Judith More**
Executive Art Editor **Janis Utton**
Project Editor **Julia North**
Editor **Michelle Pickering**
Layout Design **Martin Lovelock**
Production **Rachel Staveley**

A CIP record for this book is available from
the British Library

ISBN 1 84000 103 8

Typeset in Sabon
Printed by Toppan Printing Co Ltd in China

Contents

6 Foreword

8 Elizabethan and Jacobean

18 The 17thC Country House

32 English Baroque

38 The Age of Elegance

74 18thC Country

98 Baroque and Rococo

118 Regency and Empire

144 Victorian

178 Arts and Crafts

184 Directory

189 Glossary/Bibliography

190 Index

192 Acknowledgments

Foreword

We first published *Period Style* in the late 1980s, at a time when interest in historical styles of interior design and decoration was just beginning to mushroom. The immediate and subsequent success of the original title has reflected and contributed to not only the enduring appeal of the subject matter, but also the substantial increase in the numbers of homeowners and interior designers wishing to draw inspiration from the rich and varied vocabulary of decoration and ornament cultivated and enjoyed by previous generations. *Period Style* has thus become even more relevant and useful today, and is likely to remain so for the foreseeable future.

With this in mind, we have decided to re-model the original title by sharpening the focus on the core period styles, and by introducing many new images that will better convey both the overall look of, and the decorative detailing that underpins, each of the styles. We have also included a totally updated directory of manufacturers and suppliers. While these improvements are also intended to enhance the inspirational qualities of the book, and to make it even more user-friendly, they do not change its original purpose. This remains, firstly, to illustrate and describe the major stylistic movements (and their regional variations) – from Elizabethan and Jacobean through Baroque, Rococo, Colonial, Georgian, and Neo-classical Empire, Federal and Regency to Victorian and Arts and Crafts – that gradually became fashionable in Europe and America from the beginning of the 16th century to the early 20th century; and, secondly, to suggest the most practical and effective ways of recreating these styles nowadays.

As before, we achieve this by dividing each style section into its basic components – namely, walls, ceilings, floors, windows and doors, furniture, soft furnishings, lighting and decorative and useful artefacts (such as ceramics, glass, metalwares and fine art) – in each case identifying the predominant trends and treatments which encapsulate the essence of the various styles.

In addition to this, in recognition of the tremendous diversity of colours, motifs and patterns employed during the different historical periods, we have also produced a sister publication – *The Style Sourcebook* – which comprehensively illustrates and describes all the fabrics, wallpapers, paints, tiles and floor-coverings associated with the particular styles. We believe you will find that it is, in conjunction with the new edition of *Period Style*, an invaluable aid to choosing the key decorative elements of a style.

Since the first issue of *Period Style*, many more people have become fascinated by the history of their home, how the rooms were used originally and how they would have been decorated. Manufacturers have responded to this, and it is now possible to buy paints, fabrics, wallpapers, tiles and flooring that are based on historic documents, in a wide variety of outlets. The interest in creating a period feel extends beyond researching the correct look for your period home. Many of the homes included in this book are brand new and the style is a pastiche, allowing the owner to create a period illusion.

Deciding on the look for your home is a major decision, but it should also be highly enjoyable. I tend to follow the advice of Osbert Lancaster: "bear in mind that decoration is at its best a game: and always avoid the fatal will-o'-the-wisp of period accuracy, ... aim instead for grand theatrical statement."

OPPOSITE "The parlour" at Lansdowne, a single-storey plantation house built in 1853 in Natchez, Mississippi, USA, has been described as the finest surviving example of a Rococo Revival Victorian parlour. Notable features include original foliage-pattern wallpaper panels by Zuber; an antique Aubusson carpet; red damask lambrequins, embellished with tassels and wire edgings and copied from the 19thC originals; and a suite of French, Rococo Revival, hand-carved rosewood furniture, upholstered en-suite with the lambrequins in red damask.

Elizabethan and Jacobean

The interior of a well-to-do English house during the reigns of Elizabeth I and James I was made mellow with carved wood, rich textiles, elaborately framed paintings and the dull gleam of pewter and polished leather. An unprecedented sense of luxury reflected both the relative stability of society and the new prosperity of the merchant classes.

Interiors were embellished with surface decoration of carved wood and ornamental plasterwork. Renaissance ideas combined with nostalgia for medieval times resulted in a cheerfully eclectic mix of Classical and Gothic decoration on furniture, panelling and plasterwork, with motifs including caryatids, Doric, Ionic and Corinthian columns, acanthus leaves, egg-and-dart mouldings and, in particular, strapwork, which imitated cut leather.

A pride in possessions was expressed by paintings, rich hangings, intricate embroideries, tapestries with leafy woodland motifs or imitations of oriental carpets (known collectively as turkeywork). Open shelf buffets – which at that time were called court cupboards – were used for the display of plate. There was a proliferation of well-made furniture in new designs and with new functions. The innovation of fixed upholstery suggested a concern for comfort. Much of the wood was vigorously carved.

Walls

Panelling This was widely used to line rooms. Hardwood panelling – usually pale honey-coloured oak – would often be a simple arrangement of undecorated square or rectangular panels set in a moulded framework.

FAR LEFT This small corner combines the features most prevalent in an early 17thC grand house. It is important to realize that these homes had wonderful rich textiles in strong colours. Plain walls were often painted – note the three-tone blue. Bear in mind that you may have to have colours specially mixed if you wish to recreate this style.

LEFT Elizabethan panelling was of a glorious honey colour, not the dark, overpowering panelling favoured by the Victorians. Tapestries and hangings can still be found at auction or in specialist shops, but they can be very expensive to restore, and early tapestries do need to be well looked after. It is worth looking at late 19thC examples.

ABOVE Parham House in Sussex belies the impression that Elizabethan houses were dark with low ceilings. These rooms have a wonderful light and airy feel. The black and white marble floor, while probably 18thC, is in keeping with the rest of the room.

ABOVE This wonderful 17thC carved refectory table with a simple bench and a set of 17thC chairs is set on solid oak floorboards against a backdrop of dark wall panels. The effect depends on the coloured patination of the various woods. There are very few totally authentic tables around: most of those that come up for sale have been made up from old wooden floorboards or even railway sleepers, but they can look good. Don't dismiss 19thC or even modern reproductions as long as they are well made. Do look for a good warm colour, as stained and polished oak can be dark and dead.

RIGHT AND TOP FAR RIGHT Panelling took many forms in the late 16th and early 17thC. Old panelling can still be acquired from specialist dealers or architectural salvage yards but do ensure that it will fit the room before you purchase it. Some firms also produce reproduction panelling – look for depth of colour and good strong carving. In this early period, chairs were still reasonably rare, joynt stools and benches being the norm; however, most people find these quite uncomfortable, so for comfort's sake look for any plain 17thC chair and add tapestry cushions or stuffed leather seats.

FAR RIGHT MIDDLE AND BOTTOM Plain floorboards do add to the general Elizabethan feel, but they are not always practical. Instead of using rushes on the floor, choose one of the many types of rush matting. This period demands candlelight. However, well-concealed modern spotlights can be used to pick out details. Rush lights were one of the earliest forms of lighting, but wrought-iron chandeliers with simple decoration are perfectly in keeping. Original chandeliers can be copied by any proficient blacksmith. Ensure they are not too perfect, as a little unevenness gives a better impression of age.

ABOVE If you are buying reproduction furniture, it is essential to buy faithful reproductions and to check for good deep colour and sharp clear carving. Everything in this shot is a modern copy by Stuart Interiors, from the reproduction 17thC Derbyshire chairs to the delft plates.

OPPOSITE This superb room at St Mary's in Bramber, Sussex, was painted for the visit of Queen Elizabeth in 1585. It is an exceptional example of early *trompe l'oeil*, executed by an itinerant Flemish painter-stainer. The coffer is genuine 16thC, but the chair is a 19thC copy of a 16thC model – obviously much less expensive than the genuine article. Of the two pewter tankards, one is old, one is brand new, but both complement the room beautifully.

Panels were sometimes carved with a variety of motifs, and the more elaborate linenfold, which was carved to imitate softly draped linen, was a popular alternative. Plain panelling might be relieved by a carved frieze or might incorporate a carved fireplace mantel supported by caryatids or Classical columns with a panel depicting an allegorical subject above it. All panelling in its original state would have been much, much lighter than it is today – what we see has been darkened by age or by Victorian woodstain.

Detail might be picked out in coloured paints or inlay. Softwood panelling was almost always painted – perhaps to imitate a hardwood.

PAINTING The plaster in unpanelled rooms was frequently painted and sometimes divided horizontally into dado, infill and frieze. Walls and woodwork might be painted to resemble more desirable and expensive materials such as walnut, marble, stone or fabric hangings. Walls might also be covered with geometric patterns, often interspersed with flowers.

WALLPAPER The earliest known English printed wallpaper dates from 1509. At this time papers were designed as separate panels. By about 1600, linked repeat patterns were printed. Designs of shields, vases and flowers – motifs which also appeared on plasterwork – were usually printed in black on white. Additional colour might be added freehand or by stencilling. Paper was sometimes pasted directly onto the wall, but was more often pasted onto linen and then attached to wooden battens, or just nailed to the wall with copper tacks.

TEXTILES Patterned tapestries were popular status symbols for the rich. As these were not usually custom-made to fit a particular room, they would often overlap the wall and be taken around corners: it was quite usual for a tapestry to extend across a doorway, which might have been a little inconvenient but did help to keep out draughts. The hangings on the bed might match those used for the walls. As in earlier times, walls in less grand houses were hung with painted cloth.

CEILINGS

In the grander houses, beams would now be concealed by decorative plaster ceilings. Elizabethan plaster ceilings are usually composed of fine-ribbed, often geometric designs. In the early 17th century, broad, flat bands of strapwork were common. Repeat patterns were cast from reverse moulds; details were usually modelled by hand and painted.

FLOORS

Wooden floors were common, particularly for upstairs rooms. They might be of oak or elm – both very hardwearing – or of imported fir. Boards were generally much wider than today, but floors would often be made up of boards of different widths. During the reign of James I, parquet floors or coloured stone paving became fashionable in grander houses, and flagstones began to be used at about the same time.

FURNITURE

There was more furniture in the home than previously, and it was more luxurious and comfortable. Oak was the first choice, but beech, walnut and chestnut were sometimes used. For the rich, the medieval practice of painting and gilding the wood continued; even oak might be painted red, blue, green or black. It is difficult to know what the original colour of unpainted oak furniture would have been. While it was certainly waxed or oiled, and sometimes limed to darken it to a mid-brown (unlike the pale limed oak of the 1920s), we can be fairly certain that it was not stained black as the Victorians would have us believe.

Some pieces – especially tables, beds and cupboards built to impress the guests – were large and heavy, featuring rich carving in an amalgamation of Renaissance and Gothic motifs or with strapwork decoration.

The most important piece of furniture was still the bed. The wooden canopy which in medieval times had been suspended from the ceiling was ousted by the four-poster. Before the 16th century was out, this in turn was superseded by a bed with a carved headboard supporting the canopy at one end and two posts supporting it at the foot. An alternative type of bed had a very light framework, but elaborate hangings.

As in medieval times, stools and benches were the most usual type of seating. Some joined and turned chairs were also made. Around 1600 a new

type of armless chair appeared: the back-stool or "farthingale" chair (named after the cumbersome skirts that were worn during that period) had both seat and back upholstered in turkeywork, leather or cloth. This was the first time that fixed upholstery appeared.

Tall cupboards with doors, called presses, were used for storing clothes, linen, books and valuables. Better-quality chests were joined rather than planked. There was also a type of chest with a drawer at the bottom. Three-tiered open court cupboards, perhaps incorporating a drawer, were used to display plate. Food was stored in ventilated closed cupboards built into or hung on the wall. In households where a room was specifically set aside for eating, frame tables on fixed supports were usual. In humbler households and for servants, trestle tables were the norm.

A fairly common piece of furniture was the versatile bench table; the hinged back could be swung over to turn bench into table.

Accessories

Tablecovers and cushions added to the comfort and, along with tapestries and hangings, helped give a soft luxurious appearance to an interior in which there were large expanses of wood.

Pewter was widely used for plates, spoons, drinking vessels, candlesticks and so on. There were also some beautiful objects made in silver – salts, ceremonial cups and flagons engraved with designs based on Flemish and German originals.

Glass vessels, for most people, were made of thick green, cast Wealden glass, although the rich enjoyed delicate Venetian glass, or imitations of it made in England by migrant workers from Italy.

Pottery was often of mediocre quality and would be used for tableware only by the poor, though good, cheap black-, green- and yellow-glazed ware was available. The rich might have stoneglazed wares imported from Germany, Islamic pottery or Chinese porcelain, perhaps mounted in silver.

Clocks were very rare until the end of this period. Early on there were brass-cased table clocks and iron wall clocks; later brass-cased lantern clocks were hung on the wall.

OPPOSITE TOP LEFT Period interiors have a special feel about them when most of the elements come from the same era. This 17thC Flemish needlework armchair blends perfectly with the 17thC furniture and panelling. (The table lamp is made from a 17thC candlestick and a pleated parchment shade.) The design of the textiles is also typical of the period, with roses, irises and carnations worked mainly in pink, indigo and blue-green. The original vegetable dyes keep their freshness, whereas the more modern aniline dyes tend to fade. Some fabric companies produce reasonable machine-made copies of early fabrics, particularly flamestitch. It is also possible to find hand-woven examples, but these are expensive. A good alternative, particularly for a cushion or stool cover, is to buy an early pattern with, if possible, vegetable-dyed wool and embroider it yourself.

OPPOSITE MIDDLE LEFT The solid wooden look of an Elizabethan bedroom can be enlivened by the use of fabrics. Crewelwork is particularly effective. Early crewelwork is difficult to find, although most major auction houses now have textile and costume sales and most major cities have specialist textile dealers. There are also modern reproduction fabrics – good ones will echo the deep natural colours of early textiles.

OPPOSITE BOTTOM LEFT Some of the hand-stitched silk draperies on this spectacular Elizabethan bed at Parham House in Sussex are traditionally ascribed to Mary Queen of Scots but could equally have been worked by her sister-in-law, Marie de Medici. The textiles comprise cream satin embroideries worked c.1585; the Mary Queen of Scots needlework on the coverlet, back, canopy and top testers; and the curtains and mattress valances of Hungarian flamestitch, worked c.1615.

OPPOSITE RIGHT An Elizabethan or Jacobean look can be created with a tapestry or a length of fabric with good strong colours hung on plain walls. Archways can also be hung with tapestries, which serve a dual purpose of adding colour and cutting out draughts quite efficiently. The Regency low chairs flanking the fireplace are from the Maharaja's Palace in Hyderabad, but they seem at home here, as does the Great Dane on his woven blanket.

ABOVE The main factor that gives this room its authentic turn-of-the-century feel is the rough, off-white plasterwork and the tapestry hanging. The bedhead is a later copy, and the furniture rather mixed in date and provenance, but the overall feel remains early 17thC.

RIGHT The Great Hall in Parham House in Sussex embodies the essential elements of the Elizabethan interior – bleached oak panelling, pewter plates, 17thC leather buckets and portraits of the highest quality.

Creating the look

COLOURS Deep jewel colours – glowing reds, blues, greens, yellows – are a foil for oak furniture.
WALLS If you are lucky enough to have wood panelling, consider stripping off any dark varnish and waxing the wood to a mellow gold. This will make rooms considerably lighter and less sombre. You could also install softwood panelling and paint it a strong colour (blue, red or green), or grain it to imitate a hardwood. As in a medieval house, you could hang walls with fabric – woodland tapestry-style fabric would work well. Wallpapers would have been used by this time, so you could choose a simple monoprint of shields, vases or flowers.
FLOORS Wood flooring – polished boards or parquet – or stone paving suits this style.
FURNITURE Oak is the most usual wood for furniture of this period and there is a fairly wide range of suitable styles to choose from. Look for pieces with quite elaborate turning and carving – stools, benches, chairs, court cupboards, press cupboards and chests. Wood furniture can be painted if you wish. This is the right setting for upholstered, low-backed "farthingale" chairs covered in leather, or fabrics with the appearance of needlework or oriental carpeting. Look for 19th-century "Elizabethan" reproductions; they are less expensive than the real thing and, in general, very well made. Avoid crudely carved "Jacobethan" hybrids.
SOFT FURNISHINGS Tapestry and tapestry-style fabrics, velvets, damasks and Jacobean-style crewelwork help to build the picture, and so do oriental rugs used as tablecovers. Curtains are not authentic to this style but are a necessity for most people. Choose plump cushions with tassels at each corner to soften hard seating.
LIGHTING Free-standing or ceiling-hung iron or wooden candlebranches and candlesticks are appropriate for this style and can be supplemented with subtly concealed electric lighting. Rustic-looking electric fittings in either wood and metal might also serve.
ORNAMENTS Display pewter plates, dishes, candlesticks, dark green or fine-blown glass and green-, black- or yellow-glazed pottery. Silver and Chinese porcelain or Islamic pottery is correct for this period, although they would have been available only to the rich. Oil portraits work well in this style of interior, adding to the richness of colour and texture. Add bowls of sweet-smelling pot pourri and pomanders to give the authentic scent of the age. Then all you need is a crackling log fire and some harpsichord music, madrigals or a Gregorian chant on the hi-fi. Such details always help to create an authentic ambience.

ABOVE Superb woodcarving embellishes these Jacobean chairs and the "melon bulb" legs of the Elizabethan draw-table. The large leather ale-flask and horn beakers on the table provide added authenticity. A similar composition could be achieved with 19thC reproductions.

The 17thC Country House

Several distinct influences from overseas affected the decoration of English rooms in the middle years of the 17th century. These gradually percolated through from town to country and provincial homes. From France came a fashion for decorating whole rooms en suite – with hangings, tablecovers, upholstery and so on all matching.

Inigo Jones' visits to Italy allowed him to observe Classical architecture, as well as the buildings of the 16th-century architect Andrea Palladio, at first hand. His more correct interpretation of the Classical Orders was expressed in a new concern for overall proportion. Although Jones' work was largely confined to the Court circle, his ideas did gradually spread.

Trade between Britain and the Protestant Low Countries resulted in a cross-fertilization of ideas on furnishing and furniture making, contributing toward a plainer style of furniture.

Early in the century chinoiserie and so-called "Indian" styles became popular in aristocratic circles thanks to the importation of a whole variety of items from the Far East. Among them were lacquerwork furniture, boxes and

ABOVE This corner of a landing is an excellent example of 17thC country house style. The bronze bust of Charles I, displayed in the characteristic niche at the end of the hallway, and the Carolean open armchairs, set against light panelling, give an instant feeling of the age.

RIGHT There is more to creating a 17thC country look than merely buying the right furniture: there are also the colours, textures, sounds and scents to consider. Here, the warm glow of fruitwood chairs and the rich patination of an oak table are intensified by the dull gleam of pewter, the flickering light of the candles and the generous profusion of flowers and fruit.

screens which inspired "japanned" pieces by English and Dutch craftsmen.

WALLS

PANELLING This usually entailed small units of equal size covering the entire surface. Inigo Jones, with his strong emphasis on Classical proportions, sought to change that, and his work is well illustrated by his Haynes Grange Room, now in London's Victoria and Albert Museum. This room, inspired by the Pantheon in Rome, has no skirting: pine boards run from floor to cornice, punctuated by Corinthian pilasters. More pilasters flank wall niches, fireplace and windows.

Meanwhile, in the homes of the less wealthy, traditional softwood panelling might be grained to simulate expensive hardwoods such as walnut, or marbled or tortoiseshelled, or decorated to resemble lapis lazuli. Alternatively, it might be simply painted over with a pale colour.

Venetian-style paintings might be incorporated into the panelling of a room.

WALLPAPERS These were often printed to imitate expensive textile hangings: there were damask patterns and Irish stitch (flamestitch) designs as well as florals. Papers were printed to look like wainscot panels, marble and turkeywork.

TEXTILES Any interior of any standing, if not panelled, would be decorated with hangings. These might be made of silk damask, brocatelle, worsted or woollen cloth but were more commonly of a much cheaper, coarser fabric, woven with a repeat pattern; this pattern is known in England as Dornix.

Such fabrics were woven in narrow widths, which meant that they could be seamed together to fit a particular room; sometimes two colours would be alternated. The complete hanging would then be surrounded by a border, and the joins covered with a galloon or a silk or metal lace. Hangings of gilt or embossed leather were also fashionable, the designs often showing Moorish or Islamic influence.

Tapestries continued to be used for walls, bedhangings and so on. It was not usually possible to fit tapestries to a room quite so neatly as other fabrics, because they were bought ready-made.

Sometimes, however, the very grand would have rooms specifically designed to accommodate an existing set of tapestries.

Windows

Curtains were still not common and their role was simply to keep out sunlight. This function might also be served by a "sash" – a frame with paper, linen or silk stretched over it.

Where curtains were used, they were not treated lavishly. As with bedhangings, a single curtain would be hung from a pole on rings and drawn to one side when not needed.

Floors

Strips of rush matting, like hangings, might be tailored to fit the room. The standard type was thick and heavy and held the dirt, but there was also a finer, lighter, more decorative type imported from Africa. By this stage oriental rugs might well be seen on the floor rather than on the table.

Ceilings

Under the influence of Inigo Jones, many fine plasterwork designs in geometric patterns started to appear on the more expensive ceilings. The squares, ovals or circles of the designs were sometimes filled with paintings.

Furniture

Life was definitely becoming more comfortable. The most usual type of chair was upholstered, and was based on the back-stool of earlier times. Larger versions with higher seats and arms were used for the most important member of the household or for a visitor. Often such "great chairs" would have matching footstools, and the same basic design was used to make couches.

OPPOSITE The interior of Frog Pool Farm, a medieval house in Avon, England, has been restored and decorated in 17thC country style. Characteristic elements include the exposed wooden beams, the flagstone floor, the wooden plank door with its arch-top stone surround, and the scrubbed, pale terracotta-coloured limewash finish on the walls. The walnut table is 17thC. However, the Windsor chair is actually 18thC.

BELOW TOP LEFT Naive animal paintings are typical of the era. These candlesticks are 17thC Italian. The early 18thC provincial dresser harks back in style to the 17thC.

BELOW BOTTOM LEFT This exotic corner has been created with a solid Charles II chest and a screen made from a 17thC Dutch oil painting.

BELOW CENTRE Good 17thC furniture calls for simple arrangements to display it to best effect.

BELOW Wrought iron, plain woods and a naive painting on a stark white wall – an embodiment of 17thC country style. All the furniture here is original.

LEFT The sitting room of the home featured on these two pages is a comfortable and relaxed interpretation of 17thC style, which successfully incorporates a modern settee and a glass central table into the design.

BELOW This set-piece is typical of 17thC groupings – note the way in which the paintings are hung on the wall, the grouping of the Qianlong "laughing boy" figures and the straightforward arrangement of the late 17thC chairs and the William and Mary double lowboy.

OPPOSITE A magnificent collection of mid-17thC French walnut furniture on a white Amtico vinyl tile floor – an interesting juxtaposition that works well. The collection of Kangxi porcelain is arranged in typical 17thC Dutch manner. When buying Chinese porcelain, look for a rich colour of blue.

Upholstery fabrics included turkeywork, velvet, leather and plain cloth, depending on the pocket and taste of the owner.

Provincial homes might have the old-fashioned heavy oak, panel-back chair which continued to be made well into the next century. There were also simple chairs, with or without arms and often painted red, green or black, which had turned members and rush seats. Both rush seats and solid wooden ones might have down-filled cushions with a tassel at each corner.

The gate-legged table and the chest-of-drawers made their appearance in the middle of the 17th century. In the dining room, as well as the necessary table and chairs, there would be a cupboard or buffet for plate, possibly with each open shelf covered with a linen cloth.

The bedroom continued to be the most important room in the house, and the bed might well be fitted with hangings matched to those on the walls. Dressing tables began to be seen. These would have floor-length tablecovers or carpets with a small top-cloth of linen.

LIGHTING

Rooms were still lit by candles or simple oil lamps. Table candlesticks in the larger houses would be of brass and in the humbler ones of pewter. Candles were also carried in wall sconces, backed with a brass, tinplate or mirrored plate to reflect the light.

ACCESSORIES

Brass and silver were increasingly used for domestic implements during this period – fireplace furniture, chandeliers and so on. Trumpet-based brass candlesticks are typical.

ABOVE In a corner of this sitting room stands a pair of absolutely authentic 17thC Venetian chairs which have been re-covered in a modern flamestitch fabric.

The early American home

Not surprisingly, the early colonists built, furnished and decorated their houses to resemble those that they had left behind. Although wealthy English people settled in Virginia, settlers came mostly from small towns and rural areas of Germany and the Low Countries as well as Britain, and were able to bring little with them except tools; therefore, houses and furniture had to be made with materials that were to hand. In the early days, settlers had to find what shelter they could, but by the middle of the 17th century it was fair to say, of New England at least, that "the Lord hath been pleased to turn all the wigwams, huts and hovels the English dwelt in at their first coming, into orderly, fair and well built houses, well furnished many of them". These houses might be of timber, brick or stone.

Despite regional variations, a large proportion of the interiors of the time reflected the English influence. "Well furnished" they may have been, but to modern eyes they would be utilitarian and lacking in comfort.

WALLS AND FLOORS

The boards which made up the structure of the house might form the interior surfaces of the rooms as well. In the better houses, walls might be plastered and whitewashed, or clad with vertical boards which helped to keep the house warmer. In the Hart Room of New York's Metropolitan Museum of Art – an authentic re-creation of the period – three walls are plastered and whitewashed, while the fireplace wall is clad with boards decorated with a light moulding at the joins. Floors would be nothing more than bare wooden boards at this time.

FURNITURE

Settlers were not often people of fashion, and in any case new ideas were slow to travel across the Atlantic. Locally made furniture of native woods, often oak, reflected the styles current in Europe a few years earlier.

Chests, which could be used for both storage and seating, remained necessary pieces of furniture from the earliest times. These chests often had carved decoration, with different regions favouring different patterns.

Trestle tables were common where rooms had to serve several purposes. For the same reason, fold-up tables and frame tables with detachable tops were popular. Small occasional tables served a number of purposes. Another useful piece when space was at a premium was the hinged-back chair, sometimes with a drawer under the seat, which converted into a table.

Stools and benches were the usual seating, but three types of chair were made locally. The first two both had turned members and wood or rush seats: the Brewster armchair had a double row of spindles in the back and more spindles below the arms and under the seat, while the Carver was quite a simple affair with a single row of spindles in the back only. The third, or Wainscot, chair was an imposing piece with a panelled back and wooden seat. Later, toward the end of the century, the more comfortable "Cromwellian" chair – the type of back-stool preferred by Cromwell, with upholstered back and seat – made its appearance.

Court cupboards and press cupboards to store household goods and to display plate and pottery were important items in any household, and toward the end of the century they became very elaborate showpieces.

ACCESSORIES

Textiles were used to bring comfort and colour into rather spartan interiors. Well-padded cushions in woollen cloth, ornamented with large tassels, softened the wooden or rush seats of chairs. Examples of the art of patchwork and quilting were displayed throughout the home.

An abundance of suitable clay made it possible to make pots, pitchers and so on for general household use; these were often embellished with slip or sgraffito decoration. The shape and decoration varied from place to place. The Pennsylvania Dutch made particularly attractive wares with naive designs of birds, animals, flowers and leaves. Pewter was also used for household objects, and craftsmen worked in silver from quite early on.

BELOW This 17thC room from a house in Wilmington, Massachusetts, is absolutely authentic, from the solid simple furniture and the plain off-white walls to the hint of concern for creature comforts evidenced in the padded seat cushions.

OPPOSITE This room from New Hampshire is from the very early 18thC. It is panelled with feather-edge boarding that has been painted. Early paintwork had a streaked effect – this wasn't deliberate, but was due to the composition of the paint – so a perfect modern finish would look quite wrong. The panelling itself is easy to copy. The banister-back chairs are perfectly in period, as are the delftware plates which are contemporary English copies of Chinese porcelain originals. Horn beakers, while you wouldn't want to drink out of them every day, nor put them in the dishwasher, contribute to the mood and are still quite inexpensive at auction.

ABOVE This authentic painted dresser dates from c.1700 but it is a country piece, and country furniture tended to lag several decades behind the times. If you want to give furniture an antique painted effect, then this is the model from which to draw inspiration.

RIGHT This is a room in a Victorian terraced house with a distinct 17thC country look about it. The mood has been achieved by a clever use of colours, a couple of ingenious 17thC carved and gilded panels teamed with a modern American paper frieze, solid-looking furniture and a faded Persian carpet. The spongeware on the dresser dates from the 19thC, but it fits in perfectly with the 17thC look, as do all the other simple country hand-worked pieces.

FAR RIGHT TOP AND BOTTOM Here are two other views of this delightful room, which is bursting with conversation pieces. The eclectic collections are all based around the same theme of hand-crafted country pieces.

RIGHT TOP This wonderful 17thC country furniture is enhanced by the choice of paint colour and textiles. The disguised wardrobe has been created by hanging a pair of matching 19thC patchwork quilts in place of doors.

RIGHT BOTTOM Against the excellent background colours, this Elizabethan four-poster gets its country feel from the mix of fabrics. The crewelwork hangings are original but 19thC copies would look as good and some modern Indian fabrics would give a similar effect. Patchwork always looks right for country styles of any period. The ottoman is covered with a kelim – you could use a damaged kelim in this situation.

OPPOSITE The essence of 17thC country style is conjured up in all the elements here – the colours, the original painted dresser, the brightly coloured 19thC spongeware, the earthenware, the rush light holders, the samplers, the naive painting, the prints and the chandelier – which is a modern copy of a 17thC original.

OPPOSITE This room gives an overall impression of 17thC country style while retaining elements of modern comfort – a perfect compromise. A large tapestry dominates the room, Chinese porcelain is much in evidence and the modern carpet is mostly hidden by a Persian rug. Of course, coffee tables were not a feature of 17thC homes, but they do seem to have become an essential for modern life – this clever solution comprises a sheet of plate glass resting on a quartet of cast lions.

Creating the look

This is a relaxed style that is suitable for beamed cottages and/or houses of modest pretensions. The style can be easily adapted to bring the same homey feel to buildings of other eras.

COLOURS Slightly faded colours suit this style – almost as though the rich Elizabethan fabrics had been exposed to sunlight for some time.

WALLS Paint these white or in a soft shade to complement other colours in the room – peach, cream or apricot suit this mellow style.

FLOORS Polished boards, sisal matting or flagstones have the right feel for this period style and can be topped with oriental rugs in faded tones of pink, turquoise, blue and beige.

FURNITURE Pieces at this time were well-made, but less heavily ornamented than Elizabethan and Jacobean pieces. Supplement fine original or reproduction pieces with appropriately styled pine furniture that has been given a distressed paint finish. Gate-legged tables of the 1930s can work just as well as original 17th-century ones.

SOFT FURNISHINGS Printed Jacobean design, flamestitch patterns, embroidery, old-looking velvets and faded silks work well.

LIGHTING See Elizabethan and Jacobean, page 17.

FINISHING TOUCHES Brass candlesticks would look good with the mellow polished furniture. There was a growing interest in all things Eastern at this time, so lacquerwork boxes and screens would be appropriate.

Music to set the mood for this style would include Vivaldi's *The Four Seasons*, Bach's *Brandenburg Concertos 1–6*, and Vaughan Williams' delightful *Fantasia on Greensleeves*.

ABOVE LEFT AND RIGHT Set on a mid-17thC dresser, the display of delft, saltglaze and earthenware ceramics, interspersed with artefacts, illuminated with candles and enlivened with flowers and fruits, is highly evocative of 17thC interiors. Also typical of the period are the roses arranged in a 17thC pewter jug – pewter being the third most prestigious metal, after gold and silver, at this time.

English Baroque

RIGHT The Baroque feel of this magnificent dining room is mainly achieved by the deep turquoise panelled walls, the ornate cornice and the gilding. Panelling at this period was more prominent, with more panels, especially on doors. Rooms often contained niches for displaying porcelain or busts. The chairs and table here are early 19thC, but their sturdy form fits well with this style in this setting.

RIGHT Dennis Severs has turned his City of London home into living history. This ground-floor receiving room is an authentic re-creation of the Restoration period. Note the dark painted walls and floor, the low level of light and the paintings lit from below. It is worth remembering that all paintings were bottom-lit – and were painted with this in mind – until the advent of electric lighting.

The emergence of the flamboyant English Baroque style coincided with the restoration to the English throne in 1660 of the equally flamboyant Charles II after 11 years of staid and serious Commonwealth. The version of the Baroque that developed in England under Charles II and matured in the reign of William and Mary (1689–1702) came partly direct from France but more strongly via Holland.

The Baroque is a style of theatrical grandeur, of swelling curves and massive forms. Rooms now looked very different from those of previous eras. The basic shell was often rather sombre, but the effect was offset by the glowing jewel colours of painted ceilings, tapestries and upholstery and by the gleam of silver chandeliers, silver-decorated furniture and mirrors.

Queen Mary had developed a passion for oriental porcelain and blue-and-white delftware while living in Holland, and she started a craze for collecting these pieces when she came to England as Queen. Displays of blue-and-white wares became as typical a feature of an English room, and later of an American parlour, as they were of a Dutch one. The greater sophistication and comfort of the William and Mary style reached America just as the era was coming to an end in England. The American version of the style lasted roughly until the mid-1720s.

Walls and ceilings

The rooms of great houses were often panelled in oak. This was the high point of woodcarving in England. Motifs were frequently carried out in pearwood or limewood, then applied to oak panelling. Pine woodwork was frequently painted to look like marble, rockwork or a finer wood such as walnut.

PLASTERWORK During this period great advances were made in plasterwork with the development of a harder, quick-drying plaster, *stucco duro*, which made it possible to create elaborate naturalistic motifs similar to those found in woodcarving. By the end of the 17th century, however, elaborate plasterwork was giving way to the new vogue for painted ceilings.

HANGINGS FOR WALLS These were now often decorated with a fringe along the top and bottom and down the edges.

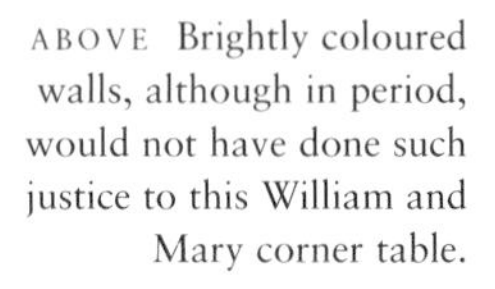

ABOVE Brightly coloured walls, although in period, would not have done such justice to this William and Mary corner table.

ABOVE Choosing a suitable fabric for early upholstered furniture is not easy. Flamestitch designs tend to work on any early chairs.

BELOW This corner of Dennis Severs' receiving room (see p.33) houses just a fraction of his fine collection of 17thC Restoration artefacts. This is not an age of pristine refinement – there should be scattered ashes in the grate and candlewax dripping over candlesticks.

RIGHT A panelled room has been painted in tones of light burgundy. It makes a striking background for the 17thC lacquer chinoiserie side chairs and the massive 18thC blue-and-white vases and covers. Symmetry is the essence of English Baroque in the grand manner.

Leather hangings were particularly popular for dining rooms because they did not absorb smells.
WALLPAPER Hand-painted papers from China were considered the height of fashion. Block-printed papers were locally produced in rolls.

WINDOWS

Curtains began to take on a more important role. They were often hung in pairs in the 1670s and soon rod and rings were disguised by a pelmet, which became the chief focus of decoration.

FLOORS

Parquetry was sometimes used in grand settings. Persian, Turkish and Savonnerie carpets were now commonly seen on the floor, and turkeywork was used for carpets as well as for upholstery.

LIGHTING

Rooms were brighter at night than they had been, since people tended to burn a greater number of candles. Candlestands had come into fashion, and chandeliers were hung quite low.

FURNITURE

Walnut ousted oak as the fashionable wood at this time, and pieces were often inlaid with marquetry. There was a passion for decorating furniture with silver, and some pieces were completely encased. Oriental lacquer was fashionable, and screens were often cannibalized to make cabinet furniture.

The same basic shapes of furniture came into fashion in America. Pieces were imported and then copied by local craftsmen. On the whole the native product was more restrained than the original models. Corner cupboards and occasional tables were in demand to display collections of imported ceramics, and bedhangings were elaborate.

ACCESSORIES

The fashion for tea, coffee and chocolate required new types of pottery and silverware. Forks became usual in fashionable circles. The Restoration was a very prosperous time, and silver was used for all manner of pieces. Owing to advances in English glass, glass goblets were ousting silver for wine – which must have improved the taste considerably.

RIGHT Sometimes even a hallway or an alcove can convey an immediate sense of period. This late 17thC chest-on-stand is in a hallway facing the front door.

BELOW An alcove on a stairwell houses a period piece – a late 17thC chest, framed by a suitable swag of fabric over the window.

RIGHT This dining room has elements from many periods but its basic feeling is that of English Baroque. The chairs are 19thC copies of 17thC style – always a good buy, as early chairs are expensive and tend to be too fragile for everyday use. The Rococo carved and gilded wooden brackets are originals; however, quite good modern Italian copies are not too difficult to find.

RIGHT This is a harmonious blend of authentic antiques with well-made, properly researched reproductions. The bureau is a country piece from the early 18thC, the chair is a modern reproduction William and Mary, the tyg (drinking vessel) is dated 1700 and the slipware candlesticks are new.

Creating the look

Walls Large oak panels framed with moulding or pine panelling painted to look like marble or walnut are both authentic treatments. If you can't afford the real thing, you could divide a plain plastered wall into sections edged by mouldings and then give each "panel" a suitable *faux* finish. Another approach would be to use pine panelling painted with a distressed finish – one tone rubbed or dragged over a very similar one works well. You could cover panels or whole walls with damask or moiré stretched onto battens, covering the nails with fringing in the manner of the time. Yellow is a pleasing background for collections of blue-and-white porcelain.

Floors Use oriental or Savonnerie-style carpets on top of parquet or polished boards for an authentic look.

Soft furnishings Suitable fabrics include damask, moiré and silk. You might use a linen-weave with a block-printed chinoiserie design. You could hang curtains from rods and rings or top them with a fringed pelmet.

Furniture Walnut is the wood for this era. Choose narrow high-backed chairs with scrolled legs and carved tops. Barley-twist legs are also right for the period. Chair seats and backs might be caned or covered in needlework or cut velvet. Swing toilet mirrors on box stands are very characteristic. Choose chests-on-chests raised from the floor on turned legs. Victorian furniture called "Elizabethan" was really in the style of William and Mary: this would certainly be less expensive than original pieces. Look too for lacquered chinoiserie pieces and screens.

Lighting Candlelight was still the only form of illumination. Silver candlesticks, chandeliers and wall sconces are correct, but you can compromise with silver-coloured reproduction electric fittings, or better still install concealed uplighters with soft peach-coloured bulbs.

Above A perfect set-piece of English Baroque style: a 17thC Portuguese table adorned in the appropriate manner with a range of Kangxi and Qianlong porcelain, set against a wall of brilliant yellow.

Ornaments Blue-and-white Chinese vases and jars massed on shelves over a fireplace, on tables, on top of cabinets and on wall brackets give a feeling of the age. An abundance of silver is characteristic, and lacquered boxes would reflect the fascination with the Orient.

Finishing touches It was fashionable to display a large piece of oriental porcelain or delftware vases on the stretchers under a cabinet. For a similar effect place a large vase or ginger jar under a side table and match it with a collection of blue-and-white jars and vases on top.

The music of the Baroque period is a bit of an acquired taste – try Pachelbel's *Canon*, the various song collections of Purcell and his *Funeral Music for Queen Mary*. There is a CD, *Baroque Favourites*, which includes works by Pachelbel, Purcell, Vivaldi, Bach, Mouret and others.

The Age of Elegance

Queen Anne occupied the English throne for just twelve years at the beginning of the 18th century. This was a time of transition from the flamboyant English Baroque to the Palladianism of the Georgian era. Interiors became plainer and both furniture and metalwork styles were simpler and more elegant.

Queen Anne

Despite the fact that no great innovations were made in architecture or the decorative arts during Queen Anne's short reign, the period has become synonymous with all that is desirable in elegance, comfort and good taste. This was the time of a domestic, understated English style typified by a rather gentle, domesticated Queen.

The era is characterized by a greater simplicity, with emphasis on first-class materials and workmanship. The beauty of a piece of furniture derived from its shape and from the figuring of the wood and simple veneering, rather than depending on marquetry, carving and ornament. The same applied to silver and to brass: decoration was often limited to simple engraving and appliqués.

The Duchess of Marlborough, friend and confidante of the Queen, summed up the commonly held desire to "have things plain and clean, from a piece of wainscot to a lady's face".

American Queen Anne

The quiet elegance of the Queen Anne style spread to America but did not become current until well after the Queen's death. The second quarter of the 18th century is the age of "American Queen Anne". As in England, the most characteristic features of the style were its overall elegant simplicity and the cabriole leg, which appeared on furniture such as chairs, sofas, tables, low- and highboys and so on.

The Dutch influence was still very much in evidence. Hand-painted delft tiles were imported from Holland and often used to decorate fireplaces. A type of large painted cupboard, typical of the New York area, was based on a Dutch style but had grisaille decoration instead of the fine woods and ornate carving of the original.

ABOVE The 18thC was the age of elegance and opulence – or rather of opulent effects achieved with imagination and flair rather than by an ostentatious display of wealth. This four-poster has been created from a divan, using floor-to-ceiling posts, lengths of moulding and masses of fabric, tassels, bows and braids. Even the fancy scrolls are simply the cardboard centres of kitchen rolls, covered in fabric. The fine collection of Chinese porcelain is in fact a motley assortment from many periods – some of the pieces are quite badly damaged.

LEFT Subtlety is not a vital ingredient of early 18thC interiors. This corner is delightfully overdone, with rich fabrics everywhere and a mirror with crewelwork overframe: crewelwork applied to a plain frame can achieve a convincing effect. The collection of items on the table, including feathers, vinaigrettes and brushes, all add to the sense of profusion.

BELOW In the same bedroom as that depicted on the left, an early 18thC chest-on-stand, framed by an unusual display of blue-and-white porcelain on gilt brackets, stands out against the pale blue walls. The interesting display on top of the chest has been kept firm by gluing various pieces together; obviously this is not recommended for fine, early porcelain.

OPPOSITE The plain panelling in this room has been painted a wonderful warm shade of deep chestnut, which is ideal at night-time and very cosy in winter, but could be rather dark during the day, particularly if the room is north-facing. The scallop-shell candle shields are an inventive touch. The magnificent garlands are made of nuts threaded through chicken wire and varnished.

BELOW LEFT The elegant lines of early Georgian furniture look particularly good in a context of pale yellows, emphasizing the sense of quiet comfort inherent in the style.

LEFT CENTRE This wonderful example of an early 18thC walnut dining chair covered in opulent red damask demonstrates the superb craftsmanship of the period. The style has been much copied, both in the 19thC and today.

LEFT These Queen Anne-style chairs are an unusual addition to a Regency country kitchen where rustic chairs would have been more orthodox. The chairs have been painted, which makes them look less formal, and they fit in very well. The paint also hides the fact that the chairs were bought as singles, not as a set.

LEFT In this New York apartment on Park Avenue, beautiful pieces of Queen Anne walnut furniture create the style. The placement is absolutely right, as symmetry was very much a theme of the age. The flower watercolours are also in period – these are originals, but there are some very good prints around.

ABOVE CENTRE An early 18thC silver table, authentically crammed with 18th and 19thC silver boxes, makes for a pretty, feminine interpretation of the style. The casual bunch of sweetpeas sets it off perfectly.

ABOVE RIGHT The mixture of 17th and 18thC furniture sits well in this 16thC interior, the choice of fabric helping to create a sense of harmony. If you can't find or afford original needlework, there are plenty of good copies to be found.

Creating the look

Colours Hues were quite strong and dark in the early Georgian interior. Paints were limited to olive greens, browns, greys and off-whites, and the colours of printed fabrics were mainly reds, browns, purples and blacks. Silks and velvets added rich reds, greens, blues and golds.

Walls If you are lucky enough to have an early 18th-century house with its panelling intact, you are halfway to creating an authentic "feel". If not you might consider having plain pine panelling installed to divide the walls into three areas – dado, infill and cornice. Incorporating cupboards, arch-topped niches and fireplaces into the panelling is correct for the period. Panelling can be grained to simulate a more luxurious wood, or it can be painted – grey, brown or olive green are suitable colours. An imperfect "dragged" paint effect in two closely related tones works well. If you do not wish to go to the expense of having a room panelled, you could simulate panelling by applying moulding, then painting in an appropriate colour.

Floors A large rug is a better choice than a fitted carpet – an oriental design works particularly well. Originally a rug would have been placed on top of plain, scrubbed boards. This is not a popular choice today: instead you might prefer to sand, seal and polish your floorboards, or perhaps darken them with a woodstain, coloured varnish or gloss paint. If you do not have a wooden floor, or want a warmer look, you could cover the floor with a sisal matting and use rugs on top. Also correct is floorcloth – canvas painted with a geometric pattern.

Soft furnishings Damasks and velvets suit this style, as do coarser cotton fabrics with a block-print design in black, dark red or brown. Brightly coloured printed fabric was not readily available at this time.

Shuttered windows can be left uncurtained in a room in this style, but the effect of this can be rather bleak. A better choice is to hang full-length curtains from a pole or, as would have been fashionable at the time, to cover the "workings" with a pelmet. Self-coloured woven damasks based on 18th-century designs are widely available and are a good choice for upholstery. You might like to copy the practical Georgian habit of covering fine upholstery with slipcovers in an everyday fabric. Striped ticking, which can be bought in a number of different colours, looks most attractive when used for slipcovers. Alternatively, you might like to use it for the actual upholstery.

Furniture Choose pieces with the cabriole legs characteristic of this time: dining chairs, upholstered wing chairs and sofas, writing tables, dressing tables, chests-of-drawers, as well as chests-on-chests, dome-topped bureau-cabinets and bureau-bookcases. These may be in walnut – characteristic of the Queen Anne period and early reign of George I – or mahogany which replaced it. In a less formal setting choose more robust "country" pieces in oak which have the same, although heavier, lines.

Georgian furniture is expensive, but you can pick up single chairs at auctions and make up your own sets. Reproductions made in the 19th century look better than modern ones, as they will have acquired a certain patina of age. If you want to mix in modern furniture – which can look stunning if done with sufficient conviction – choose pieces with a fine, elegant line. Bauhaus-inspired pieces can look good in a Georgian setting.

Ornaments Pictures in gilt frames – portraits, landscape paintings and hunting scenes – suit rooms in this style. Hogarth was beginning to make a name for himself by the late 1720s and prints of his *Beggar's Opera* and *Rake's Progress* also help create the mood.

Genuine 18th-century porcelain and pottery is very expensive, but a collection of pottery with simple blue-and-white patterns reminiscent of the delftware of the time make a good substitute. Use an informal vase of flowers to fill a fireplace opening in summer. Mirrors played an important role; look for small wood-framed mirrors with arched tops.

Opposite This room is coloured with confidence. The nut garlands, ornate ceiling, pilasters and candles make a major contribution to the mood. Ladies used fans to screen their faces from candles and firescreens to obscure the hearth. This was partly to protect their eyes from the glare but also to prevent their thick wax make-up from melting.

Right Another view of the same room. Authentic touches include lavender swept into the corners, and oranges and cloves in dishes. Tea-making was by now a major social ceremony, and here we have all the artefacts, including early English porcelain cups and saucers.

Lighting Don't light rooms too brightly – candles would have been the only source of illumination at the time. Use them where you can with candlesticks in brass or silver. Electrified chandeliers are produced, but give a much brighter light than candles ever did. Electric table lamps give attractive pools of light: choose classic candlestick or oriental ginger jar shapes. Supplement these with wall-lantern styles and mirror-back sconces. Dimmer switches for centre lights or table lamps help in creating the right atmosphere.

Finishing touches Whether or not you decide to panel a room, it is worthwhile building in an arched niche on either side of a fireplace, with panelled cupboards underneath. Originally such niches would be used for a bust or statues but today they might display porcelain.

RIGHT A well-researched early Georgian smoking room recreated in Dennis Severs' City of London home. The placement of the furniture (the chairs are modern copies) takes its cue from the period painting over the mantelpiece. This is a dramatic room, with the main focus of attention on the artfully arranged drinking vessels, bottles and bowls.

OPPOSITE This close-up of the room shown on the left reveals a streaked, nicotine-coloured finish to the walls. Note the attention to detail here – the mantelpiece display that sets the scene so perfectly. Many of these items can be purchased quite inexpensively in provincial auction sales and even car boot and garage sales.

Early to mid-Georgian

While the wealthy homes of Europe were awash with Rococo swirls, England was going very much its own way. The gracious and elegant Palladian style of the middle years of the century was inspired by a reappraisal of the work of the Italian architect Andrea Palladio and his English disciple Inigo Jones.

A wall in a typical Georgian Palladian room would be divided into three – the dado, the infill, and the frieze and cornice – corresponding to the division of a Classical column into base, shaft and entablature. The same principle was applied to the fireplace. Mouldings played an important part in these rooms. They were used to create the friezes and cornices, to decorate the coffering of ceilings and to ornament doors, windows, fireplaces and large furniture. Repeat designs include dentil, egg-and-dart, Greek key, acanthus leaf, Vitruvian scroll and bay-leaf garland.

Symmetry and balance were the keynote of such a room: a niche with a statue or bust on one side of the fireplace would inevitably be balanced by another on the other side. The newly fashionable combination of console and pier glass would be symmetrically placed. Rooms were still formally arranged, with furniture set back against the walls.

Interiors contained less wood than formerly. Principal rooms in fashionable houses came to be decorated with plasterwork instead of wood panelling. Floors covered with large carpets were becoming more and more usual and for the first time curtains played a major role in decoration. One of the great changes was in the colour of wood furniture – it was now rich brown mahogany instead of golden walnut.

Strong colours were usual in a Palladian interior. It was not until the middle of the century that paler colours became fashionable.

In the 1740s, signs of the asymmetrical Rococo style, typified by the S-curve, began to influence Georgian interiors. It did not permeate the style of whole rooms. Rococo motifs might sometimes be incorporated into plasterwork. More often, however, Rococo elements were seen in smaller decorative pieces – in girandoles, mirrors and brackets, in furniture decoration and in silver and porcelain articles. Typical motifs were the small shells which might be found in rock pools, lightly drawn acanthus leaves, ribbonwork, plants, flowers, festoons and waves.

At the same time chinoiserie, another style fashionable on the Continent, was becoming the rage in England.

The mid-18th century saw an enthusiasm for everything Chinese which had little to do with China, but was in reality a Western vision of an exotic, little-known country, Cathay – a sort of willow-pattern-plate world. Chinoiserie pagodas, pavilions, dragons and mandarins worked well with the asymmetry and writhing lines of Rococo and were often combined with them, particularly in plasterwork and carved wood. There was a great deal of chinoiserie furniture – cabinets topped by pagodas and so on – and the style was sometimes adopted for whole rooms to charming, if slightly dotty, effect.

BELOW The early Georgian era still had a rustic feel about it, especially in ordinary middle-class homes where a fireplace full of ashes and broken clay pipes would have been a common sight, and would not have been thought untidy.

Gothick was another style that came into fashion. A purely English phenomenon, this was about as close to the real medieval world as chinoiserie was to China. It manifested itself in mock ruins and quirky garden buildings as well as in interiors and, occasionally, whole houses. It called for Gothick objects and, of course, appropriate furniture. Window tracery, pinnacles and crockets appeared on otherwise standard Georgian cabinets, bookcases and chairs.

ABOVE A touch of whimsy on the wall of the same room as that shown in the picture on the left. A lot of the fun in creating period styles comes from scouting about to find small items from your chosen period and arranging them as a set-piece on a shelf, a mantel or a wall. Here, an 18thC style tricorn hat and plaited wig add a quirky touch to this re-creation of a gentleman's dressing room.

Walls

Wood panelling started to wane as a fashion in grander homes. Instead, the walls of principal rooms were decorated with stucco. They might also still be hung with textiles – silk damask, velvet and so on. The fabric was usually nailed to battens and the nails hidden by decorative fillets of carved and gilded wood, gilded or painted papier mâché or gilt leather.

Wallpaper, like textiles, was frequently used for ladies' apartments. Flock wallpaper became very fashionable at this time.

Ceilings

Coffered plaster ceilings, ornamented with Classical mouldings and complemented by Classically inspired cornices and friezes, were usual for this period. Often they were decorated with gilding. Ceiling and wall decoration might be executed in papier mâché.

Floors

In grander houses floors were often carpeted. As well as oriental rugs and Savonnerie ones imported from France, there were patterned Axminster carpets. Wilton cut-pile carpeting would be joined in strips to make large carpets and then finished with a complementary border.

Much less expensive was a type of carpeting that had no pile and was reversible, known as Scotch carpet or "listed" carpet. It was woven from strips of cloth and could be used as runners or joined to cover larger areas. Another inexpensive floor covering was floorcloth – canvas painted with a simple geometric design.

Windows

Curtains were now a usual feature of a room. If textiles were used to cover walls, the curtains would usually be of the same fabric; in a bedroom they would frequently match the bedhangings. Festooned and draped curtains were more fashionable than simple paired arrangements.

BELOW AND RIGHT Here are more examples of an early Georgian mantelpiece and tablescape that go a long way toward creating the feel of the times. The delftware items here are English copies of the extremely popular Chinese porcelain of the period – note the naive quality of decoration.

Furniture

Large pieces of furniture, such as bureaux and bookcases, show a strong architectural influence in their design and ornament. Console tables are very characteristic of this time. They were supported by brackets at the back and by a single front support, which would usually be an elaborately carved and gilded affair; typical subjects were eagles or dolphins. The tops were usually of marble or scagliola (imitation marble).

Thomas Chippendale is particularly associated with the mid-1700s. Although his workshop was relatively small, his book of designs, *The Gentleman and Cabinet-Maker's Director*, was highly influential.

The wood usually chosen for chairs and cabinet furniture at the beginning of George I's reign was walnut. Then, in the 1720s, mahogany – a wood hardly seen before in England – began to be imported. Mahogany was stronger, less affected by worm and more suited to carving than walnut, and the trees were bigger, making it possible to cut larger planks.

BELOW This is a convincing example of panelling painted to emulate a grained wood effect. Again, small-scale still-life set-pieces on the mantelpiece and side table are all-important in establishing the appropriate atmosphere.

BELOW This interesting interior combines rich drapery with simple matt painted walls, country chairs and plain stained floorboards. The oak gate-leg table is actually Edwardian but painted a Georgian green. The candelabrum is a modern copy.

ABOVE A Georgian feeling is re-created here with comb-effect painted panelling acting as a backdrop to typical furniture of the period. The chairs are originals and have the ball-and-claw feet which were prevalent at this time.

The cabriole chair leg which came into fashion in the reign of Queen Anne continued to be popular for some time. The graceful curve of the leg affected the shape of the whole chair, which was more curving than before. The knees of such chairs were often carved with smooth oval cabochons; seat rails might be ornamented with lion or satyr masks. Cabriole legs were finished with different types of feet at different times, but the most enduring was the claw-and-ball foot. Cabriole legs were also used on tables.

From the 1730s chairs became squarer-looking, and had wider backs with a bowed top rail. The upholstery of seats, backs and arms was square-edged to suit the shape of the chair, unlike the stuffing of French upholstery which gave a domed outline. Loose covers in striped or checked linen were used to protect expensive upholstery fabrics, and were removed only for very special occasions.

The wing chair continued to be popular until the middle of the century, when it went out of fashion. There were folding dining tables, with flaps supported on swing legs. At first these tables were oval, but later they were usually rectangular, which made it possible to place several together to make a long table.

Tea tables continued to be fashionable and might be rectangular or round, often with a gallery around the top. There were also special small stands for kettles.

Accessories

Busts, costly porcelain figures and delftware displayed on wall brackets and chimneypieces were very much in vogue.

Tea caddies were an essential part of the English tea ceremony: containers, often of silver, were stored inside a decorative box which was usually locked. This was opened up with due ceremony and the tea mixed and made at the table. Landscape paintings and portraits depicting the sitters in their homes became popular.

OPPOSITE The look in this dining room is typical of a middle-class home of the period. Carpets would not be appropriate, but rugs could be thrown over the varnished floor for a warmer, more comfortable look.

BELOW Strong matt green painted panelling and black painted floorboards create an effective background for a fine portrait and a beautiful chair. The window drapery here is purely ornamental – internal shutters keep out the light.

ABOVE An elegant display of rusticity can be consistent with an authentic Georgian look. Painting the insignificant table the same colour as the panelling is a clever idea which works perfectly on this occasion.

RIGHT Shutters dispense with the need for curtains in this dramatic wine-red sitting room – the perfect setting for the Georgian furniture. Nothing is over-done: this is a comfortable, lived-in room. The oak child's chair is a genuine country piece but looks quite at home in these elegant surroundings.

BELOW This relaxing sitting room with rough, painted walls and decorative drapes has a distinctly Georgian feel. The shutters and window frames have been painted with an interesting two-tone streaked effect which complements the colour of the room. The chandelier is 18thC in style.

RIGHT This homely little corner, painted in two shades of green, has a Georgian ambience despite the presence of a radiator.

FAR RIGHT This bed, in a very small room, has been constructed to fit in with Georgian-style panelling – the book shelves cut into the walls are an interesting feature, and very convenient for bed-time reading.

BELOW The three-tone paintwork gives added prominence to the panelling in this comfortable, intimate room. The arrangement of pictures is typical of the period – note the run of prints on the right and the plates "hung" on a strip of fabric that can be glimpsed in the Chippendale mirror.

ABOVE No one would guess that the location of the sitting room shown here and on the right is an apartment on Park Avenue, New York. The style of Chippendale furniture featured here is often referred to as "Chinese Chippendale", and is regarded as some of the finest English furniture ever produced. Elaborate curtains with intricate pelmets are very much part of the late Georgian style. On a practical level, it is worth having roller blinds hung discreetly behind the drapery, as drawing such curtains tends to ruin the form.

RIGHT The pilaster, cornice and door frames are all applied mouldings. The dramatic colour scheme is a bold alternative to the safer pale green or magnolia paintwork so often associated with this type of setting. Note how the comfortable modern seating blends in with the overall period effect. In this apartment, each major room is in a different period style – you can glimpse the Art Deco room through the open door.

Mid- to late Georgian

By the end of the 1750s there was a reawakening of interest throughout Europe in the Classical world. Excavation at sites such as Herculaneum and Pompeii built up a more authentic picture of life in an ordinary Roman household and revealed that interiors were decorated in a much less rigid and more flowing style than had been previously thought, with painted decoration as valid an element as mouldings and stucco. This evidence, together with the discovery of many well-preserved everyday domestic articles, had a great impact on late 17th-century interior design.

The most important figure in developing the English version of Neo-classicism was Robert Adam, who dominated interior design in the years 1760–90. An aspect of Adam's vision new to English decorating was his concept of an interior and its furnishings as a coordinated whole. In an Adam room the design of floor, ceiling, walls and furniture is all closely related. The Neo-classical style of Adam is much lighter and more elegant than the Palladian. He aimed "to transfuse the beautiful spirit of antiquity with novelty and variety".

Neo-classical motifs used in painting, plasterwork and furniture include acanthus and laurel leaves, festoons, guilloches, medallions, urns, rams' heads, tripods, gryphons, curling arabesques, sphinxes, lyres, the husk, anthemion (honeysuckle) and palmette. Many Adam rooms are in the "Etruscan" style – painted with figures based on Greek red-and-black figure pottery (it was thought at the time, erroneously, that these pots were made by the Etruscans).

Colours generally favoured by Adam were pale green, blue and pink, although some colour schemes remained surprisingly strong; the breakfast room at Osterley Park, Middlesex, for example, has bright yellow walls with blue papier mâché borders and white woodwork.

Delicate plain furniture, either painted or in satinwood decorated with marquetry and inlay, is typical of this time. Pottery and porcelain shapes were plain and elegant and based on antique models.

WALLS AND CEILINGS

The architectural elements became less dominant in Neo-classical rooms – cornices, friezes, mouldings and relief decorations were now noticeably shallower and more delicate.

The ceiling was the most important feature of a room, according to Adam. It might be decorated with plasterwork and/or painting, and the design on the ceiling was often echoed (not exactly copied) by that which appeared on the floor. Plaster decoration for both walls and ceilings was the distinctive feature of many rooms and was very often white.

Walls might be painted a single plain colour and decorated with a border. The wall above the dado was sometimes divided into panels ornamented with scrolling acanthus foliage, perhaps with specially commissioned small paintings incorporated into the design. Alternatively, a white stucco dado rail, border and frieze, and roundels and rectangular panels of Neo-classical motifs, might be set against a single-colour background.

BELOW This panelling, taken from a 1700s house in Colchester, Connecticut, shows the influence of the Classical period, particularly in the broken pediment and the coloured niche. The chair is a superb example from Philadelphia, c.1760.

RIGHT A late Georgian feel suffuses this room, with its pale lemon walls, niches, archways and Adam-style fireplace highlighted in white. The Regency stool and the modern armchair are quite in keeping, and the collection of mid-18thC creamware is absolutely right. To create a Georgian interior, it is not necessary to start with a Georgian room – all the architectural features can be purchased and applied to blank modern walls and ceilings.

OPPOSITE A dining room in the Classical tradition with a good beige background colour, applied pilasters picked out in beige and cream and a *trompe l'oeil* detail above the door. The table, chairs, glassware and creamware plates are all in style, and there is no conflict with the Regency chiffonier, as this period saw the birth of the Regency style.

For more modest interiors, Josiah Wedgwood sold black basaltware tablets (cameos and medallions copied exactly from Roman and Greek originals) for "inlaying in the panels of rooms ... or as pictures in dressing rooms".

Walls might also be hung with fabric in the same way as in Palladian houses, or papered, perhaps with a Neo-classical pattern.

Floors

Flooring materials were much the same as in the previous period. In grand houses decorated by Adam, the design, whether marble or carpet, would usually echo that of the ceiling. Two carpet factories – Moorfields and Axminster – produced carpets in competition with the Savonnerie carpets of France. Both produced Neo-classical designs for Adam rooms. Painted floorcloth was still used extensively.

Windows

Pairs of curtains were in fashion during this period, often topped with a festoon pelmet; these pelmets might also be used alone to decorate the top of a window. Venetian blinds were occasionally seen.

Furniture

The shapes of the Neo-classical period were simple and delicate, with straight legs. The preferred wood was satinwood – except for the dining room – and often decorated with marquetry and inlay. Much furniture was painted.

Eating and drinking was a serious business in Georgian England and one of the most important rooms in the house was the dining room. The furniture for this room – mainly a male domain – was mahogany. Adam is credited with inventing the sideboard – a marble-topped table with an urn on a pedestal at either side. Both urns and pedestals were designed to hold all the necessities of a dining room – knives, plates, water, bottles of wine and so on. Later on in smaller, less grand rooms the pedestals were combined with the table.

Adam designed the key pieces of furniture in most of his interiors. Elegant semicircular tables and commodes are typical of Adam. He also designed decorative pieces such as girandoles, urns, *torchères* (candlestands) and so on. Adam furniture was frequently gilt or painted and gilded to carry through the theme of the room for which it was intended.

Chippendale designed in the Neo-classical style and made furniture for Adam houses, but the names associated most closely with furniture for less grand homes of this period are Hepplewhite and Sheraton. Their books of designs influenced numerous furniture makers.

The typical Hepplewhite chair has a shield back decorated with Prince of Wales feathers, urn or triple lilies. Some Hepplewhite furniture is carved and painted or japanned. He also favoured elaborate marquetry decoration.

OPPOSITE Georgian style works well with the muted tones of pale green. Panelled walls give the impression of a late Georgian interior, but the furniture here spans the Queen Anne and early Georgian periods. Simplicity and symmetry are the keynotes. When you have such exceptional pieces of furniture, drapes can be quite understated.

LEFT Of all period furniture Georgian styles are the most adaptable – as much at home on a vinyl floor as on a Persian rug. Georgian chairs of totally different designs work together very well, so you can buy them as singles, which is much less expensive than buying a set.

ABOVE Plain white painted panelling from c.1700 sets off the impeccable details of this fine Chippendale furniture. The panelling could be copied using pieces of dado rail. The painted floorcloth is perfectly in period.

RIGHT The Georgians valued proportion and light much more than either their predecessors or their successors. Here, white painted windows and shutters accentuate the light and airy feeling of the room, so typical of this style.

Sheraton chairs usually have square backs with upright splats. He designed some delightful small pieces of furniture – for example *bonheurs-du-jour* (writing desks for ladies) and a version of the flap-sided Pembroke table. Many pieces are inlaid or have painted decoration.

Accessories

Josiah Wedgwood realized the importance of the new Classical fashion early on, and he produced creamware for the table in simple Classical lines which complemented the interiors and furniture designs of the day. He also produced jasperware and black basaltware which imitated different types of stone. The shapes and decoration of many ornamental pieces of jasperware and basaltware are based exactly on those of antique Roman and Etruscan (Greek) vases. Among the pieces made in jasperware were copies of the famous Roman glass Portland Vase of the 1st century BC.

Worcester and Derby porcelain in Classical shapes, often decorated with landscape views, are typical of this period.

Matthew Boulton, metalware manufacturer and friend of Wedgwood, supplied Adam with ormolu decoration for doors and chimneypieces. He also manufactured some very fine pieces in blue john stone mounted in ormolu.

Romantic porcelain figures by Meissen, Sèvres, Chelsea and Bow were also fashionable.

PRIVATE EYE
SCRABBLE

OPPOSITE Fabrics play an essential role in setting a style. Here, the drapery and the Georgian-style bookcases give an immediate feel of the age. Marble fireplaces, either authentic or reproduction, can be bought from auction houses or architectural salvage companies.

TOP LEFT AND TOP RIGHT The clean, simple lines of a modern apartment can provide an excellent setting for fine 18thC furniture. Here, the overall Georgian feel is helped along by pale colours and Classical shapes. The glass Albrizzi table, itself a classic piece, contrasts well with the Thomas Chippendale chair, one of 18 made by the designer himself for Brocket Hall.

BOTTOM LEFT This 18thC butler's tray makes an excellent drinks stand. The pile of old books is in fact an artfully disguised ice-box. Note how the flooring changes from boards to brick as you pass from drawing room to dining room – Georgian furniture looks good on either surface.

BOTTOM RIGHT A peaceful Classical Georgian mood created in a room with all the original architectural features of the period. Pale colours are very much part of this look.

Creating the look

COLOURS You can choose between a pale palette of creams, greys, pale greens and yellows or stronger colours such as rich pinks and blues, turquoise, even tangerine. Both look right in a Georgian interior.

WALLS These can be divided into dado, infill and frieze with mouldings creating the divisions and panels. They can then be decorated with paint, perhaps using two closely related tones for different areas. Broken paint finishes – rag rolling, dragging or sponging – suit this style of room. You may decide to offset coloured walls with white plasterwork and mouldings; this works particularly well if you decide on a pale wall colour.

Hand-painted Chinese wallpapers are correct, or you could choose one of the less expensive printed papers based on 18th-century chinoiserie or other patterns. Wallpapers imitating damask, silk, printed cotton and chintzes were fashionable in the 18th century, and there was a vogue for flock wallpaper. Give an authentic finishing touch by adding a gilt fillet border around the edges of panels or other areas of paper. Alternatively, walls can be covered with fabric stretched onto battens with braid covering the nails around the edges.

SOFT FURNISHINGS Suitable fabrics range from damasks, moirés and velvets to simple block-printed patterns and multicoloured designs of birds and flowers. It was customary to have curtains in the same fabric as that used on walls. Festoon curtains are right for the period, as are pairs of curtains, topped by elaborate swag-and-tail pelmets.

FURNITURE Less costly than the real thing are pieces made 100 or so years later when there was a revival of this style. Commodious wing chairs combine comfort with formality, and modern sofas with uncluttered lines will complement true or reproduction Georgian shapes. It is possible also for a skilful hand to blend frankly modern furniture with period pieces. For example, a simple chrome and glass table can set off straight-legged Chippendale-style chairs to stunning effect.

FLOORS AND LIGHTING See Queen Anne/early Georgian, page 43.

ORNAMENTS Mirrors play an important part in this type of room – both as decoration and to reflect light. Choose designs with asymmetrical Rococo decoration. Look for mirror-backed wall brackets, known as girandoles, in Rococo or chinoiserie style. Hang prints in formal groupings and balance one group with another.

FINISHING TOUCHES Copy a Georgian trick and buy sheets of printed garlands and other ornaments to create a realistic impression of *trompe l'oeil* plasterwork details, ribbons, tassels and other decorations.

Paste prints to the wall in formal arrangements and frame them with monochrome stencilled "frames" to make your own version of a period print room.

"Hang" small decorative pictures on lengths of gathered fabric, topped with bows. This is particularly effective with oval portraits.

Cover the chain supporting a chandelier with a tube of gathered fabric.

Decorate the centre of some wall panels with a large stencilled design of an urn or a Wedgwood-style cameo.

From well-concealed speakers, the strains of Bach's *Orchestral Suites* might be a good choice, or Mozart's *Symphony No. 40*, or Haydn's *12 London Symphonies*.

OPPOSITE Classical pillars used to create an imaginary division in a room are a feature of the Adam style. The symmetry is also carried through in the fireplace, overmantel mirror, rug and flanking display cabinets. Georgian furniture, over the long period of its development, was of consistently high quality and craftsmanship: this means that early Georgian pieces can be in total harmony with those of late George III. Here, the whole gamut of styles is represented, from a chair of c.1725 to a Sheraton table.

ABOVE A modern electric table lamp proportioned along Classical lines, its stem taking the form of a plinth-mounted column, looks just right among the exquisite pieces of furniture in this corner of a pale, panelled Georgian drawing room.

TOP LEFT Walls of sunshine yellow make a good background for blue-and-white porcelain and mahogany furniture. There is no need to sacrifice comfort for style – wing chairs are luxurious and perfectly in period, and modern sofas on simple, traditional lines harmonize well. The coffee table problem (they didn't have them, we need them) is here solved with a sheet of plate glass and a quartet of gryphons in support.

ABOVE LEFT In any interpretation of the Georgian look, due attention must be paid to both comfort and colour. Here, modern seating, upholstered in neutral shades, blends attractively with the panelling and the drapes. Polished floorboards with Persian rugs are a colourful option.

ABOVE RIGHT A lesson in Georgian symmetry – a well-balanced display of good furniture against a background of pale stripes.

OPPOSITE TOP LEFT A good way to treat a Georgian interior is to apply a suitable paint colour above the dado rail and white below, down to the floor. This way, you have a rich warm background for paintings and collections, and a white background to show off the elegantly carved legs of Georgian tables and chairs.

OPPOSITE BOTTOM LEFT The skilful wood-effect paint finish on the panelled walls and the highly polished floorboards superbly complement the patina and inlaid decoration of this exquisite Georgian table.

OPPOSITE FAR RIGHT, TOP AND BOTTOM This wonderfully simple Connecticut farmhouse exudes Georgian country style at its best – generous chintz curtains, bare polished floorboards, beautiful mahogany furniture, simply framed naive portraits and a profusion of flowers.

ABOVE A Georgian chest-of-drawers combines function and beauty in a way that typifies the period. A new chest-of-drawers would probably be worth only a fraction of its original price the moment you got it home, and might even fall apart within five years or so if the workmanship were not up to standard. However, a Georgian original would last many lifetimes and would certainly increase in value.

ABOVE RIGHT A simple late Georgian chest flanked by two lovely chairs and a symmetrical arrangement of prints – the essential Georgian statement.

OPPOSITE TOP In this bedroom, the striped walls and the simple lines of sofa, chairs and table are unmistakably Georgian in feeling. The distinctly Victorian bed adds a stylish dash of surprise and shows that it is perfectly acceptable to mix period styles.

OPPOSITE BOTTOM LEFT This is a New York apartment. The Georgian style has been achieved with a couple of original pieces of furniture, clever use of fabric and a good sense of detail. The Empire-style bed canopy introduces a note of contrast.

OPPOSITE CENTRE Obviously, the concept of a Georgian bathroom equipped for modern convenience is a contradiction in terms. However, if you are trying to conjure up a period mood among present-day porcelain and plumbing, carry through the colours and the draperies used in the bedroom and choose perhaps one item of period furniture. This pretty piece is a late 18thC Pembroke table adorned with a collection of small porcelain pieces and silver boxes.

OPPOSITE FAR RIGHT This bedroom shows how Georgian can work as a feminine style – the pale colours, quilts and sprigged fabric are in sharp contrast to the dark tones of the furniture.

LEFT The 18thC mahogany tilt-top table in this American dining room is perfectly complemented by a set of 20thC reproduction, Georgian-style chairs.

BELOW Pink-red painted walls provide an harmonious backdrop for a George III dining table, chairs, glass-front display cabinet and sideboard – all of red mahogany and the latter displaying a selection of lustrous Georgian silverware.

OPPOSITE LEFT Much of the elegance of Georgian interiors resides in the fundamental symmetry and simplicity inherent in Georgian furniture. Here a fine George III mahogany sideboard plays host to a pair of high-quality George III mahogany knifeboxes.

OPPOSITE RIGHT (TOP, CENTRE AND BOTTOM) Whether illuminated by daylight or candle light, creating an authentic period look is heavily dependent on an appropriate use of colour. In these three interiors the Georgian style is established not only by period furniture, but also by the pale green and muted yellows enriched with pinkish-reds and/or warm mahogany browns.

ABOVE LEFT Hallways are intended to create a strong first impression – here, stripped pine, peacock blue walls, a plain stone floor, a collection of decoy ducks and various other paraphernalia create a Georgian country feeling.

ABOVE RIGHT Walls the colour of crushed raspberries help to enliven the formal atmosphere of this symmetrical marble-floored hallway. The orange tree sentinels add to the symmetry and also add an outside/inside dimension.

OPPOSITE A strongly Classical interior reflects the transition from late Georgian to Regency style. The painted floor echoes Classical designs, and the painted walls effectively imitate stone. The urn shapes and the subject matter of the painting are consistent with this return to Classicism. This ensemble has been created not in a grand Georgian mansion but in the hallway of a New York apartment.

American Federal

The War of Independence interrupted the flow of new ideas from Europe to America. Consequently, it was not until the 1790s that Neo-classical influences began to be seen in America.

Houses were now more spacious, with lofty ceilings and large windows which often extended down to the floor in the French manner. These well-proportioned interiors were well suited to the modified version of the Neo-classical style current in America in the Federal period, which spans the years from 1790 to about 1810. Toward the end of the period, influences of the incipient Greek Revival style could be seen.

WALLS AND CEILINGS

These were more simply decorated than in Neo-classical rooms in England. The ceiling would probably have a central plaster rose. French scenic wallpapers were popular.

WINDOWS

Formal swag-and-tail or draped pelmets in silk were seen in Federal-style rooms, used often over simple muslin or fine cotton curtains.

FLOORS

Hand-knotted carpets produced in Philadelphia in the 1790s were made in strips which were joined. Painted floorcloths, sometimes with patterns imitating Turkey or Savonnerie carpets, were used.

BELOW The simple expedient of placing one good period piece in a hallway can set the tone for the whole interior. This small Federal-style settee shows the influence of Sheraton.

BELOW This warm, matt painted dining room embodies the essence of Federal style – note the stencilled floor and the painted display cupboard. The Sheraton-style fancy chairs date from c.1820. The flexible dining table is a Federal double D end – in this photograph the two D ends have been placed together to form an oval and the centrepiece is being used as a sideboard to the left of the picture. The Colonial brass chandelier is a reproduction. The painting, dated c.1795, is a naive work from the Hudson River School. The porcelain is a mixture of English Newhall and Chinese export – all from approximately the same period.

OPPOSITE LEFT The Deer Park Parlor in the American Museum in Bath is a typical late 18thC interior from Baltimore County, Maryland. You can see the strong Adam influences in the proportions and moulding, especially in the fireplace surround. The furniture with its inlays and veneers shows the influence of Sheraton and Hepplewhite. The bookcase is from Boston and is made of mahogany and pine with bird's-eye maple veneer and border details of rosewood. The wallpaper, with its motif of ears of corn, is a French paper made specifically for the American market, which by now was of great significance commercially.

TOP RIGHT A simple wallscape redolent with Federal detail. Note the stencilled floor, the matt painted panelling, the original painted Sheraton fancy chairs, the William IV cut crystal, marble and glass lustres (slightly later but they fit in well), the Hudson River School painting and the beautiful Federal tiger maple and bird's-eye maple card table – probably made in Massachusetts around 1790.

CENTRE RIGHT A pleasing mix of English and American furniture is shown in this house in Southport, Connecticut. The two corner chairs are English, c.1790, the tripod table is American and the wonderful paired Pembroke tables are from Baltimore. The mirror on the right of the picture is Queen Anne, the one on the left American Federal.

BOTTOM RIGHT An American interior decorated in turn-of-the-century style. The stunning drapes are not for drawing but for decoration only, their fanciful headings echoing the swirls atop the mirror. The deep, rich tones of mahogany furniture look magnificent against a background of neutral colour.

FURNITURE

The pattern books of Hepplewhite and Sheraton with their modified versions of Adam style were widely used by furniture makers in America. Frequently, elements from different books of design were merged together.

The United States had no great national centre of fashion and culture comparable with Paris or London in Europe. This resulted in furniture with different regional characteristics. The best painted and japanned pieces came from Baltimore; inlays in light wood and areas of painted glass are typical features from this area. Typical of New England was the Martha Washington, or lolling, chair, based on earlier French and English open armchairs.

New pieces at this period included the tambour desk, sometimes with a bookcase on top. Many new types of table and sideboard were being made.

ACCESSORIES

Shapes of silverware exhibited the straight sides and symmetrical curves of the Neo-classical style. In the Metropolitan Museum's American Wing a Federal tea service has the pieces in urn and helmet shapes with eagle finials. Candlesticks would be of simple column shapes. Presentation pieces were fashionable and again would usually be based on antique models.

The popular tableware designs of Wedgwood were imported from England. Trade with the East was now flourishing, enabling oriental porcelain in Neo-classical shapes made for the Western market to be a common feature.

Ornamental chandeliers and candelabra decorated with glass drops were imported from England to complement the formal style of decoration. Mullet-branched candelabra frequently had cut and engraved glass shades.

OPPOSITE This stencilled bedroom in the American Museum in Bath is an excellent example of the wall and furniture decoration popular in the early years of the 19thC. A journeyman artist would have painted this – arriving with his dry pigments and paper stencils, he would have decorated the house in exchange for board and lodging. The small chairs would have been bought from a "Yankee peddler" who distributed goods from the back of a wagon. The canopy bedstead which dominates the room is authentically hung with hand-worked lace and dressed with an embroidered quilt.

ABOVE Canopy bedsteads were popular well into the 19thC. Lace hangings give the bed a light and airy feeling, as do the simple country flowers and the plain white walls. The patchwork quilt is a distinctly American touch which can be copied using one of the excellent modern patchwork quilt kits.

TOP RIGHT This exceptional American walnut bed, c.1780, with drapes that accentuate its linear style blends perfectly with the pair of English mahogany commodes and the French lyre-back chair, all from the closing years of the 18thC.

ABOVE This late 18thC canopy bed is in a lovely small country house in Connecticut. The simple country chest is c.1800, and the bench by the window is actually a seat from a horse-drawn sleigh. The country feeling is unmistakable – polished boards, unlined curtains and a simple rug are all that is required to set the scene.

18thC Country

RIGHT If you do not have the time or patience for ragging or dragging your walls, you can use one of the many ragged, dragged or sponged-effect wallpapers. This one is by Osborne and Little. The plain floorboards and painted furniture all add to the country feel. The old coffer was repainted in a naive style in the early 20thC. As a general rule, don't ever strip any furniture with original paintwork, just enjoy its lived-in looks. The chair in the foreground is late 18thC French provincial.

LEFT Broken paint finishes are an important part of any early country style. The two-tone vanilla sponged effect produces a suitably faded appearance. Polished boards are perfect for this style.

OPPOSITE An early country kitchen is no place for fitted units, but this practical arrangement is a good compromise. These dresser-type units have been cleverly distressed with a streaked paint finish and the country mood is further reinforced by rustic antiques.

In country and provincial districts, styles in furniture and decoration were more informal than in cities. Even when urban fashions filtered through to country areas, they tended to appear in a more robust form than originally. Change for fashion's sake was not common. Wood panelling, for example, remained popular in the country long after it had lost favour in town. Furniture was chunkier and sturdier with less refined decoration, in keeping with a more rustic setting. Shapes originally intended to be made in walnut or mahogany might well be translated into oak.

In general, the 18th-century country style followed the basic principles of symmetry and balance of the Georgian interior, but the whole feeling was more mellow, more lived-in, more rustic.

Walls and Ceilings

Drawing rooms and dining rooms of the grander country dwellings were generally lined with wood panelling which was sometimes painted in pale, sunny colours. Other rooms would have limewashed walls of brick or stone or rough plasterwork and exposed beams – just as in country cottages.

Floors

Humble homes would have floors of stone or tiles, or polished wooden boards strewn with rag rugs, rush matting or painted floorcloths. Grand drawing rooms would be carpeted with maybe the addition of an oriental rug.

Windows

Again, simplicity was the keynote here. In winter thick fabrics which kept out both light and chilly draughts hung from wooden poles, alternated in the summer months with lightweight linens.

Furniture

Of course, some of the fine furniture of the Georgian period found its way into grand country homes, but in general provincial centres were making robust and simple variations that were more appropriate to country life. Typical of the 18th-century country interior are the provincial ladderback chair and the oak sideboard. The early years of the century saw the advent of one of the most useful pieces of furniture ever devised – the kitchen dresser.

FLOUR

ABOVE AND BELOW Two views of the same room in which good late 18thC/early 19thC furniture is accentuated with appropriate fabrics, rush matting and plain walls. The door curtain gives the room a cosy feeling and also cuts down draughts. Around the inglenook fireplace bare bricks add to the atmosphere, and the ladderback chairs with tie-on cushions look invitingly comfortable. Originally, a log fire would have crackled in the open hearth. The wood-burning stove is a 19thC invention: modern, efficient copies are virtually indistinguishable from the real thing.

LEFT Fitted kitchen dressers convey an immediate sense of period. The benches and plank-top table add to this effect. The butcher's block is perfectly in keeping and combines country style with practicality. The look is simple – stripped pine, bare boards and an interesting use of colour. Wild flowers and weeds in simple containers complete the picture.

ABOVE LEFT An inviting breakfast room with a distinctive 18thC feel benefits from the warmth and practicality of a modern Aga cooker backed by a collection of period tiles. Early tiles can still be bought quite inexpensively at auction sales. Collections of kitchen-related items such as pots, kettles or jugs will give such rooms visual focus.

ABOVE RIGHT This is the scullery of the room shown above left. Its practical pine units are shown off against a patterned terracotta wallpaper, and pine shelving displays collections of blue-and-white porcelain and pottery. Old ladderback chairs can be bought singly and painted and stencilled to make them look like an old and matching set.

BELOW An early country atmosphere has been created in this modern kitchen by a clever use of old pine and simple uncluttered lines. The chair, which is French, actually dates from the mid-19thC, as does the Dutch painted table, but their simple forms make them look much earlier.

RIGHT Dressers are actually very practical, providing worktop space and plenty of storage. Although they look bulky, they don't take up a large amount of space, as they are wide and tall rather than deep.

BOTTOM RIGHT This airy kitchen has been given an 18thC feeling by the matt creamy paintwork, stripped pine and polished floorboards. The terracotta colour makes the chimney breast the focal point of the room.

OPPOSITE These kitchens would fit happily into an 18th or 19thC period home, and still meet the requirements of a 20thC cook. In the top left kitchen the ladderback beech chairs and the sturdy pine dresser make for a strong early feel. The colourful pottery collection in the room shown on the bottom left is Victorian. The early 19thC French provincial pine armoire in the kitchen pictured top right displays a collection of modern pottery based on early designs. This piece, with the check wallpaper and the slate floor, evoke the no-nonsense solidity of the period country style. In the bottom right kitchen the Pennsylvania "Dutch" chairs and dresser in the American Museum in Bath show how the Americans' imaginative use of colour transformed these traditional shapes. The painted toleware on the dresser features scenes from the New World. These strong earth colours are a valid alternative to the pale faded look of the English country kitchen.

RIGHT Colonial style and English 18thC country style have many features in common: simple rustic furniture, usually made of oak, yew or fruitwood; an absence of clutter; simple panelling; open fireplaces; and plain wall finishes. One of the differences lies in the palette of colours the Americans were using: strong matt "earthy" colours, while certainly found in Europe at this time, became a key feature of the American Colonial home. Note the locally made decoy ducks and the way in which the stone hearth meets the floorboards.

OPPOSITE Strong earthy colours are set off by a roughly plastered and whitewashed wall. This looks very effective here because the rough plasterwork is obviously deliberate – unless done with conviction, this effect might give the impression that the decorators were due back next week. This room has four doors, each painted a different but complementary colour on both sides.

Colonial

By the early 18th century, America had begun to find its feet as a nation, and this self-confidence found expression in the American Colonial home. Interiors were now positively "American" in feeling – light, airy, uncluttered and colourful. There was pride in local craftsmanship, and although many furniture styles were based on English designs, the American interpretation was unmistakable. American flora and fauna found their way into textile and stencil designs and there was a growing market for home-grown ornaments – for simple glazed pottery, carved wooden bowls, paintings by local artists.

Walls

From about 1700 interior walls were plastered and painted. Some quite sophisticated panelling was also being used which might even be painted in flat colours – blue was a particular favourite – or even crudely marbleized.

Furniture

Rooms were uncluttered, and this feeling was considerably helped by a fair amount of built-in storage. Fireplaces were often flanked by cupboards with doors that matched the panelling of the walls. There were corner cupboards for storing plates and display cabinets were quite common.

The furniture of this period was quite refined and beautifully crafted. Many pieces were made using English designs, generally after their English vogue had finished. These adopted styles were much simplified and varied considerably from one part of the country to another.

Typical chairs of the period were simple wooden armchairs, sometimes with upholstered seats, although a few fully upholstered wing chairs were to be seen. Slant-fronted desks and highboys were very popular, and were made in considerable numbers in American furniture workshops.

Floors

The simple plank floors of the early American home were now often stencilled or covered with painted floorcloths or rugs of woven flax.

Lighting

Chandeliers and oil lamps replaced tin sconces and simple candle holders of earlier times. Candlesticks were quite often made of brass, as were the fire implements and irons.

Windows and draperies

Most homes had shutters on the inside of windows, and often on the outside as well. In the very best rooms, simple curtains in plain fabrics were used – they were sometimes swagged, but never elaborately. Beds were generally covered with quilts or simple coverlets, but in grand houses the master bed might be draped and covered in printed or embroidered fabric.

RIGHT The success of this delightful house depends to a large degree upon the use of colour, a beautiful blue teamed up with a milky white. Walking through the house occasions a series of sensory surprises. Contrasting colours, interesting groupings of furniture and objects seen from different angles create an exciting environment. Attention to detail is an important factor, as always. A country house style demands a profusion of country flowers, not stiff, formal bouquets, and paintings should have a simple painted wooden frame or none at all.

OPPOSITE LEFT Often the most powerful expressions of period style can be made in a very simple way. This strongly defined stairway has been painted in three tones of blue, and it nicely frames the magnificent early oak chair set against it. The oriental rug adds warmth and visual interest.

OPPOSITE RIGHT A wonderful lesson in the use of colour. The exterior timber-clad walls and the door have been painted a surprising shade of purple – reminiscent of mulberries and cream – revealing inside a hallway of warm terracotta and glowing wood.

ABOVE LEFT This kitchen achieves a period feeling without any sacrifice of modern convenience. The colour of the architraves, surrounds and practical modern units contrasts with the stark white of the walls and the open shelves. The stone sink with brass taps is a striking feature – both items can be obtained as modern reproductions.

ABOVE RIGHT The matt moss-green paint on the woodwork and corner cabinet here is a traditional type of paint with a milk base. Note that the interior of the open-shelved cabinet is painted a different colour – this is an authentic treatment. The doorway frames a perfect example of a mid-18thC Colonial dining room. The banister-back chairs are uniquely American. The balusters were first split – each one being therefore a half-round – and then the two halves were stuck together and turned as one piece. When the chair was assembled, the turned sides were placed on the outside of the chair-back, so that the inside was smooth for sitting against.

OPPOSITE This wonderful 18thC Rhode Island keeping room has been lovingly restored by Stephen Mack, whose knowledge and feel for period interiors has been developed by his work in dismantling and rebuilding period structures under threat of demolition. The room has many of the elements that help to create a warm country feel: the wide floorboards, the plain walls, the pottery, the 18thC country furniture, the wild flowers, the herbs hung up to dry, the wrought-iron cooking implements, the simple turned wood and wrought-iron chandelier. The 17thC Dutch painting is an interesting reminder that early colonists brought some of their treasured possessions with them. Note the white milk paint, flaking slightly, on the planked walls.

RIGHT This is an uncluttered style. The simple, firm lines of the 18thC ladderback elbow chair are set off by the tasselled cream muslin summer drapes. The country look is reinforced by the natural wooden floor, the off-whites and the terracotta-coloured panelling. The simple ceiling is nothing more elaborate than the underside of the floorboards and joists of the room above.

OPPOSITE TOP By keeping the walls stark white and bringing colour into the room via the painted woodwork and the wonderful 19thC quilt, this room has been made to appear larger than it actually is. The bed was designed to allow sea chests to fit under it, providing useful storage space. The basket in the window, now used to store dirty washing, is an original feather basket in which down and feathers were collected for stuffing into mattresses and pillows.

OPPOSITE BOTTOM Waking up to wonderful views is an added bonus for the owner of this Rhode Island home. The lack of curtains gives the bedroom a simple, country feeling. Of course, such an approach is feasible only where windows are not overlooked and are sufficiently well-fitting to keep out draughts. The slant-top desk dates from the 18thC and still boasts vestiges of its original red milk-painted finish. (Painted pieces are much more valuable if left alone, however tatty the paintwork.) The banister-back chair is also an 18thC original, as is the quilt over the luxurious feather bed.

OVERLEAF, PAGES 88–89

TOP LEFT The choice of paint is tremendously important in re-creating an 18thC Colonial home – the colonists worked with natural dyes and pigments, whereas modern paint technology is geared to perfect colour consistency and a perfect finish. This is a corner of an 18thC country bedroom, complete with open fireplace – a romantic addition to any bedroom.

TOP RIGHT These two sea chests provide excellent storage space while lending their rustic charm to the Colonial house. The rough-planked, white painted wall is totally in keeping. It is interesting to glimpse through, on the right, to the much more sophisticated chest-on-chest, and on the left to the early stone sink and rich-coloured units in the kitchen. Notice how good the open shelves look in this context.

BOTTOM LEFT This 18thC blanket chest with its original paintwork is an excellent example of the delightfully unsophisticated furniture of mid-18thC North America. The contemporary hog-scraper candlestick and the later onion-type lantern all add to the air of New England simplicity.

BOTTOM RIGHT Note the wonderful contrasting earthy colours here. The matt paintwork looks even better when scuffed with use.

FAR RIGHT Stark white paint throws coloured woodwork into relief and shows off the simple lines of 18thC furniture, artefacts and painting to good advantage. Here, the wooden floorboards are softened by a Persian rug, and at night the room is softly candlelit. This house is not entirely a period piece, as it is wired for electricity and the points have been cleverly cut into the floorboards – look carefully at the floor area under the leg of the little tripod table.

Creating the look

COLOURS These very simple, undecorated styles rely for their impact on the beautiful patina of old wood. Yellow, off-white, pale cream and vanilla would be suitable colours. A distressed look is definitely preferable to perfect finishes, and matt effects are more apt than gloss. Strong colours are not out of place – for example, pinky red or blue.

WALLS Dragged paint finishes, or sponged-effect wallpapers, are in keeping, emulating the coloured limewashes of the period. Around an open hearth, you could opt for an area of bare bricks or stones.

FLOORS Rush matting or bare wood floors with simple rugs (such as rag rugs) would convey the right mood. In the kitchen, you might opt for flagstones or plain rustic tiles.

FURNITURE Keep furniture simple; if you can't afford the real thing, modern furniture made from old pine is acceptable. Staple items of furniture would include simple chests-of-drawers, and Windsor and ladderback chairs. In the kitchen, dresser-type units should be chosen in preference to built-in units, and the table should be utilitarian bare wood – scratches and other marks will add to authenticity. Benches make an ideal companion to a kitchen table – or better still look for discarded church pews. Pieces with Rococo curves might work if sufficiently rustic in style.

LIGHTING Simple wrought-iron and wooden fittings can be found in present-day versions. Candlelight glittering on surfaces creates a suitably mellow atmosphere. Also of interest are tin lanterns with star-shaped holes, which give out a subdued but scintillating light.

WINDOWS Follow the contemporary practice of alternating between lightweight summer curtains (perhaps thin muslin) and heavier fabric in winter: of course, the heavier would not be necessary if you have shutters. Tassels may be used, but nothing too elaborate. An alternative choice would be simple blinds in a plain material – perhaps with subtle festoons.

BEDS Beds should be simple in style, although that does not preclude a modest form of hangings. Quilts are essential in bedrooms, adding a touch of colour and homeliness. Kits are now available for making your own quilts to historic designs. Alternatively, a random patchwork of colour and pattern will fit in well and will contribute a perfectly authentic touch.

FINISHING TOUCHES Chests, fruit and wild flowers in baskets, bunches of herbs hung up to dry, naive paintings (particularly of animals), earthenware bowls and carved decoy ducks are just a few suggestions for accessories. Open-hearth fires should be furnished with all the accompanying paraphernalia – andirons, cranks and so on.

A possible choice of music to conjure up an 18th-century country mood might include Handel's *Water Music Suites* and *Royal Fireworks Music* and Mozart's *Flute Concertos Nos. 1 and 2.*

OPPOSITE The success of the beautiful home in Stonnington, Connecticut, shown in both pictures here, is due to the combination of sophistication and simplicity. Here, the rough-plastered walls, the polished floorboards and the simple chequered rug are teamed with fine-quality 18thC American country furniture and an oil painting framed in simple style. The carved duck is an evocative accessory.

ABOVE This view shows the 18thC style at its most harmonious, with every element working towards the general ambience – light muslin drapes, simple 18th and 19thC country furniture, naive paintings in unadorned frames, rough walls, timber ceiling and distinctive pierced-tin chandelier. The flowers reinforce the mood.

Shaker

Led by an Englishwoman, Ann Lee, the Shakers were one of a number of Utopian sects which migrated to the New World. They arrived in 1774, and within a decade had established their central community in New Lebanon, New York. In their heyday, the first half of the 18th century, as many as 6,000 Shakers lived in communities as far west as Ohio.

The communal ideals of the Shakers led to a desire for uniformity of style throughout the many communities. Changes in living arrangements, even a decision as trivial as wearing braces rather than belts to support trousers, had to be approved by the central community at New Lebanon. Everything they *did* make and use, however, was of the highest quality. No kind of work was more valuable than any other, whether it was ploughing or weaving or making chairs. The Shaker creed exhorted each member to "put your hands to work your hearts to God". Work was a form of worship – the appearance of Shaker goods should be as pure and simple as Shaker prayers. Most Shaker goods reached their final design form between 1820 and 1850, when Shaker vitality and population were at their height.

The interiors of Shaker dwellings were kept light, plain and simple. Storage was often built-in, and the clever Shaker designs for walls and cupboards and smoothly fitted drawers have never been bettered. Tables and benches were unadorned and beautifully proportioned; many ingenious serving and sewing counters, desks and chests-of-drawers held necessities for indoor work. Objects that might clutter the room – hats, cloaks, tools, chairs and clocks – were hung on pegboards high on the walls. Walls and furniture were often painted in cheerful shades of red, blue, green and yellow. Figured woods were sometimes used for furniture making, and chair seats were made of cane, wood splints or multicoloured fabric tape.

The Shaker ladderback chair – harmonious and lightweight – is eloquent testimony of the sect's sensitivity to good furniture design. This was widely appreciated. Until as late as the Second World War, many Shaker goods were sold nationwide by catalogue.

OPPOSITE The Shakers made restrained use of subtle colour, as seen in this room. This bottle-green blanket box is topped by a trio of storage boxes. The Shakers piled their boxes in this way to remind themselves that life's purpose was to climb the "steps to heaven".

LEFT A yellow painted 1840s ladderback chair is hung tidily away on a peg while not in use. The three-drawer chest, dating from the mid-19thC, is a typical Shaker piece, and the interesting object sitting on the chest is a beautifully crafted bonnet block.

OPPOSITE TOP LEFT A naive country portrait of an inspiring Shaker elder in a simple maple frame is virtually the only ornament in this calm Shaker bedroom. The ladderback rocking chair is a typical Shaker piece, and the skirting board has been painstakingly painted with a feather to create a *faux marbre* finish.

OPPOSITE BOTTOM LEFT The "curly" or tiger maple ladderback side chair and tripod table date from c.1850. The design of the candlestick was first seen c.1750 and was still being produced in the 1920s. The small sewing basket is mid-19thC. Note the wide planking and soft but strong colours on the walls.

CENTRE Tiger maple beds in the Shaker tradition sit well with the simple country surroundings of plain white walls and polished boards. This bedroom exudes an almost monastic calm and sense of order.

ABOVE LEFT A later Shaker cupboard with its original red paintwork dates from c.1870. The child's chair is a little earlier. Chair rails for hanging chairs well out of the way were a common feature of all Shaker homes – they made it easier to clear the room ready for prayer meetings.

LEFT This is an example of modern built-in cabinetmaking in the true Shaker tradition. It takes up a whole wall of the bedroom shown in the far top left and centre pictures – a place for everything and everything in its place.

OPPOSITE This re-creation in the American Museum, Bath, shows the calm, spiritual feeling of a Shaker interior and the emphasis on furniture and objects that were stripped of ornament, made with patience and expertise – and always spotlessly clean. The effect is impressively refined, in the spirit of Mother Ann Lee's exhortation to her followers: "Do all your work as though you had a thousand years to live and as you would if you knew you must die tomorrow."

Creating the look

Shaker design can radiate a welcome sense of refuge from the noise and overstimulation of everyday life. For this reason it is prized by collectors the world over. Shaker furniture is shown to best advantage in surroundings which, while not necessarily as ascetic as those of a real Shaker community, aim for a tranquil purity.

COLOURS To emulate the Shaker style, colours should be clear and soft but never drab. White backgrounds will show the purity of Shaker-style furniture to good advantage, but a blue-grey colour also works well. Use accents of strong colour here and there – for example, the rich hues of natural timber. The grain of wood should be in evidence. Avoid brightly printed chintz, which will look incongruous.

FLOORS Polished wood floors scattered with rag or hooked rugs will complement fine Shaker furniture.

WINDOWS Bare windows are the authentic choice. However, for privacy you might like to add a roller blind or simple white muslin drapes. Avoid pelmets or any kind of decorative trimmings.

FURNITURE Except for commercial items such as boxes and chairs, genuine Shaker antiques are extremely rare. Most are in museums or private collections. However, many modern craftspeople have adopted principles akin to those of the Shakers and are producing Shaker-style furniture of great beauty. Fine cabinetmakers can be found to make single pieces of furniture to order. On a less rarefied plane, several furniture companies are reproducing Shaker designs in good materials at popular prices. Even the tradition of the Shaker catalogue persists – unfinished, handsome pieces of furniture may be bought assembled or in kit form to be made up at home.

FINISHING TOUCHES Beautiful utilitarian objects should be proudly displayed rather than tucked away. A collection of treen would be very much in keeping. Wild flowers would be in sympathy with the general ambience. An antique stove in the main room, or a reproduction stove, will help to reinforce the mood. A chair rail with pegs, in the Shaker fashion, is a good method of storage and an interesting showcase for a collection of objects.

Other styles of light, well-proportioned accessories, perhaps Scandinavian or oriental, might coexist well with Shaker designs, provided that they are in a suitable type of wood.

ABOVE A Shaker chair from the 1850s made of tiger maple. The feet of the chair have been fitted with small titler buttons for added support. These were normally made of wood but by the early 1850s the Shakers had patented the pewter titler button.

ABOVE A serene Shaker bedroom. At the same time as the Shakers were sleeping in rooms like this, the Victorians were hemmed in by patterns upon patterns, drapes upon drapes and a clutter of furniture. The rocking chair and rag rug date from c.1830.

Baroque and Rococo

The dynamic Baroque style developed in Italy but reached its most influential form in France under Louis XIV. Shells, acanthus leaves, volutes, garlands and scrolls were all used, as in Italy, but tempered with Classical restraint. In the reign of Louis XV the Baroque gave way to the more frivolous Rococo characterized by swirling, asymmetric forms. Both these styles, as well as the more severe Louis XVI style, were adapted enthusiastically in the later 19th century.

ABOVE Styles from different countries of Europe can be mixed together in the same room without disrupting the overall harmony of the finished design. Here, an 18thC French marble fireplace is surmounted by a late 18thC mirror and flanked by Italian *torchères* that have been made into lampstands. The impressive marble figure is ancient Roman.

RIGHT A wider view of the same room reveals a good example of Classical influence combined with the flamboyant French taste of the period. This suite of 18thC French furniture still has its original covering. The wall-hung tapestry was produced by English weavers and embroiderers at the Mortlake workshop, c.1700.

BELOW This dining room, cleverly created in a hallway, makes excellent use of mirrors and drapes. Note how the drapes look all the more opulent for lying in swathes upon the floor. The strongest influence in this room is the set of 17thC Venetian chairs, abetted by the Fortuny fabric on the wall in wonderful shades of green and gold. The light fittings are Italian – the Italians have always produced stylish chandeliers and candelabra, and still produce good copies.

OPPOSITE 18thC Continental taste is here epitomized by the window dressing, the Venetian glassware, the decorative flower painting on the panels and the massive Classical urn. The little topiaries are a whimsical touch, bringing with them a reminder of the beautiful garden that lies beyond the window.

Louis XIV, 1643–1715

Several figures are important in the development of the Louis XIV style. The first was the King himself, who from the time he actually took control in 1661 showed a close interest in the decoration and furnishing of his many palaces. The second figure was his minister Colbert who set up the Manufacture Royale des Gobelins to provide all the decoration and furnishings for the royal residences. The third influence was the designer and painter Charles Le Brun, the first director of the Gobelins. Versailles became the centre of Court life and here Le Brun created a grand and opulent setting to reflect Louis' power and prestige.

Louis XIV Baroque is typified by rich, rather sombre colours and heavy forms. Early on, only the most costly materials were used for furniture, and many pieces were made in solid silver. Alternatively, heavily carved and gilded wood was chosen. From around 1683 the style became less heavy. About this time there was a financial crisis, and the silver furniture was melted down and replaced by oriental lacquer and finely veneered furniture, intricately inlaid with tortoiseshell and brass. The craftsmen who carried out this work were known as ébénistes, and the greatest of them was André-Charles Boulle.

Régence and Louis XV, 1715–74

During the last few years of Louis XIV's reign there was a move away from the Baroque grandeur and formality that had been so much a feature of his Court, toward a lighter style of decoration which was to be influential throughout Europe. Under the regency of the duc d'Orleans this trend accelerated. The *Régence*, or early Rococo period (1710–30), is a time of transition between the solemn Louis XIV style and the full-blown Rococo of the Louis XV style.

Rococo was all about pleasure, and decorative motifs and themes reflect this – love-making, music, the countryside. Humour was another key element. Motifs included chinoiserie, turquerie and singerie (monkeys in human dress), often deployed to mildly comic effect.

Women, especially the witty and talented Madame de Pompadour, were playing an increasingly important role in social life at this time. Female influence was reflected in a more intimate, informal approach to design. Rooms became smaller; hence, smaller pieces of furniture were needed. Mirrors played a large part in these Rococo interiors. As well as the mirror over the fireplace there would frequently be matching pier glasses over console tables. Mirror glass might be used to screen a fireplace in summer, as well as on window-shutters: these were concealed during the day and slid across the windows at night. So many reflective surfaces gave a spacious airy look to rooms and made the most of the available light. To add to the effect, candelabra might be an integral part of the mirror frame. Bracket clocks, decorated with ormolu and Meissen figures, were a feature of many rooms, and the animal tapestries of Oudry were very popular. The paintings of Jean Antoine Watteau and works by François Boucher typify the spirit of the age.

Cabinet furniture of this period is characterized by fine veneers and ormolu mounts. There were several new types of commode, including the *encoignure*,

ABOVE LEFT A mixture of pieces of different nationalities looks unified against a plain, uncluttered background. The 18thC Swedish commode is surmounted by an 18thC oil painting by Karl van Loo and framed by 18thC French chairs with old tapestry cushions. The porcelain on the commode is 18thC Chinese export porcelain, which was produced in designs more elaborate than those preferred by the Chinese themselves.

ABOVE RIGHT French 18thC furniture is generally beautiful, expensive and fascinating to collect – most good pieces are signed by the ébéniste. This wonderful 18thC French commode was obviously made by a modest ébéniste as it has no signature, but it is undoubtedly of top quality. The chair is by Georges Jacob (1730–1814) who was the leading French cabinetmaker working in the Neo-classical style in the years preceding the French Revolution.

OPPOSITE TOP, CENTRE AND BOTTOM The owners of this New York apartment are serious collectors of 18thC French furniture, paintings and porcelain. The wall colour has been matched to the colour of a pair of *rose Pompadour* cupids elsewhere in the room. The carpet is an 18thC Tabriz which is perfectly in keeping with the Continental look, as is the marble fireplace. More modern is the Monet in the top picture – and the view from the picture windows.

a type accommodated in a corner cupboard and generally used in pairs, and the commode en tombeau, or *à la Régence*, which had three drawers, one above the other, and short legs.

Chairs with caned seats and backs came into fashion, usually with tie-on squab cushions shaped to fit seat and back. These chairs were made with and without arms, were curvilinear in form and had wide seats designed for comfort. There was also a new style of more comfortable upholstered chair: typical of the *Régence*, it had an exposed frame of carved wood and cabriole legs, strengthened with stretchers.

Louis XVI (1774–1785)

Even before the end of Louis XV's reign there was a reaction in France, as elsewhere in Europe, against the frivolity of the Rococo. This resulted in a backward look to the grandeur of Louis XIV's reign and a revival of interest in the Classical world. Furniture shapes became more severe – for example, the bombé shape popular in the Rococo became flattened, and curving legs were replaced with straight, tapering ones. Decorations changed too: the writhing, asymmetric designs disappeared, replaced by Classically inspired motifs. Pieces were sometimes decorated with porcelain plaques.

Porcelain and silver acquired the more restrained shapes and decorations inspired by the ancient world. The paintings of Jacques Louis David on improving subjects such as *The Oath of the Horatii* were more appropriate to this style than the light-hearted works of Watteau.

19th-century adaptations

Domestic interiors of the 19th century were deeply affected by a spirit of nostalgic revivalism. Inevitably, and especially in France, fashionable designers were drawn to the lavish furnishings of the age of the Sun King and his successors. Throughout the century there was a strong leaning toward Classicism of one sort or another, and this could be Grecian, Renaissance, Louis XV-Baroque or Neo-classical.

From the 1830s the most popular style was the Rococo, or Louis XV. Louis XIV also remained fashionable and the two styles, which should have been quite distinct, often became confused – even in France! Around 1860 these idioms were joined by another Louis style – Louis XVI – which frequently added to the confusion. Decorating in the various Louis styles involved using a fair amount of gilding. Gilt mouldings made from papier mâché or plaster-of-paris, in designs to suit the particular style of the room, were fashionable. These richly decorated Louis styles were expensive and therefore available only to the better-off. They were taken up by the wealthy throughout Continental Europe and in England.

On the whole, fashionable French houses were less over-full and cluttered than English ones, although the same type of rounded, deeply padded and sprung furniture was popular. The typical fat, comfortable, often ugly chair of the day was irreverently known as a *crapaud* (toad).

Wallpaper began to be mass-produced in the 1840s, and by the 1860s it was normal for most rooms to be papered. Designs ranged from the simplest

of printed patterns through to "satin papers", which had a shiny surface, and flocks. The most luxurious were the wonderful scenic wallpapers – the French led the field in the manufacture of these.

Parquet flooring, topped by a carpet, was very fashionable during this period. The French were considered by a contemporary writer on the subject to "have the best taste in the management of curtains". There were numerous, elaborate methods of draping windows in keeping with the various styles of decoration. These frequently involved elaborate pelmets and cornice decoration. A very simple type of window treatment, which would probably be more acceptable today, was to hang a pair of curtains from an elaborate pole and loop up the sides.

BELOW AND RIGHT Drapery can make a very strong statement in a room. Below, the generously bunched curtains have a strong Classical feel about them, helped along by the painted and gilt furniture. In picture on the right the interest is focused on the sunburst tiebacks and the plain fabric leading through to a pattern. Generous swathes of curtaining need not be made of expensive fabrics – choose artist's canvas, muslin or lining material, but opt for lots of it.

OPPOSITE TOP LEFT This room is dominated by a Renaissance figure in carved wood and given extra drama by the clever use of mirrors – large mirrors were typical of this era, as was the placing of sconces (these are Louis XVI) directly onto mirrors to double their effectiveness. Note how the wing chairs and the gilt wood chair blend well with the neutral-coloured modern sofa.

OPPOSITE TOP RIGHT The Gilt Room at Chilston Park Hotel, Kent, has been created using 19thC copies of earlier French furniture. The fabrics, which are totally in keeping with the gilt wood furniture, are modern copies of traditional designs. Notice the height of the bed – most early four-posters were this high, and the occupants needed a four-poster stool, like a small set of steps, to climb into bed.

OPPOSITE BOTTOM LEFT A Venetian bed dating from 1810 is swathed in a bedspread of approximately Venetian hues. The chairs, which are Florentine, date from 1780.

OPPOSITE BOTTOM RIGHT This very small bedroom has been given a dramatic treatment with bold drapery and interesting paint finishes. Note the Classical columns framing the door and the gilt curtain roses used as door handles.

TOP LEFT This dramatic room gives a strong overall impression of French 19thC design with its mirrors, chairs and chandelier. Key 19thC features are the festoon blinds, the massive Chinese vase lampstand and the collection of blackamoor figures.

TOP RIGHT Another view of the room shown top left. The walls have been hand-painted with a marble-effect finish, and the gesso fittings conceal wall lights.

BOTTOM LEFT The unusual tablescape here displays a good collection of French 19thC gilt wood and gilt metal objects on an 18thC English gilt wood table

BOTTOM RIGHT Goods and chattels have been carted back and forth over national boundaries for centuries, so there is nothing unusual in this grouping of a French Louis XVI-style gilt chair, a 17thC painted Italian cassone and the Hispano-Moresque plate.

OPPOSITE Flowers play an important role in the decoration of Kenneth Turner's living room. A floral artist, he understands how a profusion of flowers can set a mood, point up a colour scheme and perfume the air. A mass of lavender, like an indoor bush, fills the stone urn on the left. Also adding to the mood are the wonderful fabric on the chairs, the candles, the baskets, the dramatic busts and the bare floor.

LEFT This dramatic dining area is in fact a tiny lean-to off the kitchen. It has been given elegant proportions with clever use of mirrors and trelliswork. The unmistakable Regency chairs are totally at home with the overall 19thC Continental feeling. The late 19thC gilded wood figures are copies of earlier styles, the table has been made from an Italian candlestand and the chandelier is a modern Italian copy. The floor is of vinyl tiles but laid in the classic black-and-white style that was popular from the 18thC.

RIGHT A hallway in the grand late 18thC style has instant impact. The blackamoor figures are almost lifesize, the candelabra are extravagant and the marble-topped commode provides an exuberant centrepiece. The Zoffany wallpaper in two tones of yellow-gold provides a suitably grand background.

FAR RIGHT TOP Here we have almost the same elements as in the picture on the near right, but the feeling is much lighter, much less grand. All the pieces are later, 19thC examples, but the blackamoor figures still give an appropriately exotic feel to the room.

FAR RIGHT CENTRE The French pier table to the left of the fireplace here displays a wonderful example of the Rococo shell motif.

FAR RIGHT BOTTOM This fireplace is dominated by bronze groups, bronze and glass lustres and early 19thC fire implements. The shapes look very strong and imposing against the stark white background.

LEFT All the pictures on these two pages are of a classic William and Mary country house with a distinctly Continental air. The use of ornate drapes, Aubusson carpets on polished floorboards, Rococo furniture and indoor topiaries all add to the Baroque feel.

RIGHT These Imari and Chinese blue-and-white plates are a typical wall decoration of the period. If you decide to emulate it, remember that the plates need not be in perfect condition – they can even be modern copies – but they should be arranged symmetrically. The proportions of 18thC rooms seem to demand symmetry, but if you do want to go against the grain you will not get away with a half-hearted attempt – it will have to be a very positive statement.

BELOW RIGHT The two shades of yellow on the panelling provide a sunny background to 18thC English glassware displayed on a profusion of wall brackets. The series of modern flower paintings was commissioned by the owners and based on the flowers growing in the gardens – rather in the manner of an 18thC patron of the arts! The topiaries add a scent of box hedge and an intriguing inside/outside feel to this main drawing room.

OPPOSITE The ornate Rococo settee, magnificent swagged curtains and massive Kang Hsi vases with covers flanked by topiary sentinels are saved from overkill by the plain polished floorboards and the plainly painted walls. The vases on wall brackets reinforce the mood and symmetry of the display.

ABOVE A convincing 19thC Continental feel can be achieved by the acquisition of one good piece. This mid-18thC French Boulle bracket clock is an excellent example. It is based on a style created by André Charles Boulle (1642–1732), who was chief cabinetmaker to Louis XIV. Boulle work, as it is known, is brass and tortoiseshell inlaid into ebony in dense scrolling patterns. Most of the other items in the picture are 19thC French and are still relatively inexpensive to acquire at auction. The tiles on the wall are 19thC Chinese, and were bought for next to nothing in a job lot from a London sale room. The wall finish is a marbled paper by Colefax and Fowler.

ABOVE The Aubusson carpet sets the scene in this main drawing room in Plas Teg, North Wales. The walls are covered in a striped brocade and the stone fireplace is a 17thC original. The gilt wood wall sconces and stool give a very French feel and are in keeping with the Regency sofas in satin and moiré.

OPPOSITE A Classical French cameo in a Park Avenue apartment. The 18thC French carved fruitwood marble-topped table is flanked by a pair of 18thC chairs. The engravings are originals from Versailles. On the table sits an 18thC sandstone urn. The whole grouping is set off by the pale cream walls.

ABOVE LEFT AND ABOVE RIGHT Both of these interior details are from a New York apartment that has been reconstructed and re-furnished in 18thC French Rococo style. The painted wall-panelling above the dado in the sitting room on the right incorporates curvaceous foliate scrolls typical of Rococo architectural fixtures and fittings. Similarly ornate embellishments are evident on the frieze and jambs of the Louis XVI-style marble chimneypiece in the bedroom on the left. Also highly evocative of mid- to late 18thC French Rococo style are the reproduction documentary fabrics used for upholstery and table coverings. Most are embellished with the naturalistically depicted small floral motifs (mostly of wild flowers) that became increasingly fashionable during the second half of the 18th century.

LEFT An excellent collection of French 18th and 19thC furniture and a Chinese lacquer cabinet-on-stand is teamed up with collections of bronzes, gilt and wood to create a perfect 18thC Continental ambience, with a strong Chinese influence. Modern convenience and comfort are not forgotten: a modern sofa in neutral upholstery blends in perfectly, a coffee table has been created from cast gilt columns and plate glass, and the radiator has been cleverly and beautifully boxed in. In the foreground are the components of a typically French piece of furniture, the duchesses brise; this is a chaise, a chair and a stool which can be used separately or pushed together to make one piece.

ABOVE This pleasantly light and airy room has discreet modern roller blinds at the window which supply the necessary privacy while allowing the shape of the window to be seen to good advantage. The burr walnut table in the foreground is Charles X. The French gilt wood furniture was made in the 1920s in the Louis XV style.

Creating the look

You can create something of the feel of these rather grand styles by placing appropriate pieces of furniture – either real or reproduction – in a setting that makes the correct use of fabric and colour. All the Louis styles will take an immaculate finish but a look of faded charm is equally appropriate, especially on gilding. An effect of luxury is important to these styles, but this can often be created through judicious use of pattern and colour rather than expensive materials and furnishings.

COLOURS Strong colours – dark rich reds, greens and blues – or more delicate pastel tones will work equally well: the choice is a matter of individual taste. The bright pastel colours of Sèvres porcelain have a place here – *bleu céleste* (turquoise), *jaune jonquille* (yellow) and *rose Pompadour* (rose pink). One possible approach is to confine strong colours to fabrics and accessories, leaving wall colours more subdued. For the later period, also suitable are colours associated with the Etruscan style – terracotta offset by cream or pale shades of blue or grey. White and gold rooms flatter the charming, rather whimsical furniture and *objets* of the Rococo style.

FABRICS Rich fabrics suit these styles – velvets, heavy silks, damasks. Woven designs of flowers, pastoral subjects and animals will blend well. Particularly for a Louis XVI mood, choose *toile de Jouys* fabrics, printed with a scene in a single colour on a white ground: these are available in modern reproduction. Consider using embroideries and tapestries, or modern fabrics in designs by Fortuny. Bedhangings, generous and ceremonious, are a vital ingredient.

FURNITURE The two basic options are, on the one hand, the rectilinear veneered style; and, on the other hand, the more extravagant bombé shapes associated with Louis XV. The styles can be mixed for a more eclectic look. Imaginative versions of Baroque and Rococo furniture were made in the 19th century, and such pieces can still be acquired inexpensively. Gilded or painted pieces are appropriate to the look, although for a provincial version of Baroque or Rococo you might choose furniture in natural woods.

WINDOWS Window treatments should be relatively elaborate, with swags, drapes and pelmets. Remember that formality is not necessarily inconsistent with softness. Asymmetrical curtain arrangements are appropriate to the Rococo or Neo-rococo mood. A Regency or Empire window treatment would also blend in well with these styles.

FINISHING TOUCHES Porcelain vases displayed on wall brackets will reinforce the mood. Ornate mirrors also help, and will spread the light from candles. Classical trappings (for example, busts and statues) are in keeping, as are paintings (especially portraits) in elaborate gilt frames, or perhaps architectural drawings. Oriental touches will complete the picture – for example, a luxurious Chinese carpet and some choice pieces of blue-and-white china. Roses, in quite formal arrangements, would be the obvious choice of flowers to display in this style of room.

Appropriate music for these romantic styles might include: Fauré's *Pavanne for Orchestra*, Debussy's *Clair de Lune*, Chopin's *Ballades, Preludes* and *Nocturnes* and Johann Strauss II's *Viennese Waltzes*.

OPPOSITE A heady blend of drama and exuberance is the keynote of this style. Here, even the walls have impact with their strongly streaked finish, and the tablecloth cascades generously to the floor. Note the size and placement of the urns and candlesticks – timid gestures have no place in such a scheme.

ABOVE The feeling of an 18thC European interior is captured here in the inspired choice of fabrics. Hannerle Dehn, who designed the room, has hand-painted many of the fabrics herself. Elsewhere in the room is a stool that has retained its original 17thC fabric, but such finds are increasingly rare. Note the dramatic effect of the flower arrangements, and the Classical busts on pedestals which always fit well into this period.

Regency and Empire

RIGHT This is a perfect Regency cameo created in an alcove off a passageway. All the elements are here – the gilded leg of the console table, the black cast sphinxes, the simple urn with white flowers and the unmistakable lines of a standard Regency chair. The whole arrangement has a distinctly Classical feel.

OPPOSITE The plain walls here serve to accentuate the strong lines of the Swedish Empire style. All Empire styles have a lot in common and therefore they mix together well. This console table is Swedish, c.1820, and the portrait is of the Swedish King Carl Johan XIV – in Sweden this style is often referred to as the Carl Johan style. The pair of sphinxes is in period, as is the Italian sarcophagus on the table – a souvenir from a Grand Tour long ago.

Life in the English Regency period, which stretched from the late 1790s until the late 1830s, was more informal than previously. Rooms, often with a bay window, were smaller and had lower ceilings. Pieces of furniture, instead of being ranged around the room, were grouped close to the fireplace. Family and friends would gather around a circular table to talk or play cards. Interiors were much better lit than before: the new, efficient oil lamps enabled several people to share a table for reading or writing.

Regency rooms were on the whole light and graceful with fairly plain walls in a clear pale colour. There would be a narrow frieze, and the ceiling was usually plain or decorated with a small central garland with a chandelier hanging from it. Fabric was used in abundance – swathed and draped over pelmets and sometimes festooned between the legs of chairs.

Regency taste had turned away from the late Adam style and the spindly elegance of Hepplewhite furniture. A new late Neo-classical manner was in vogue. This placed the emphasis on a much stricter Classicism of form and shape rather than on mere ornament – as had been the case with Adam. Late Neo-classicism had much in common with the French Empire style which existed alongside it. The major influences were the civilizations of Ancient Greece and Egypt. Furniture based on ancient models was rather heavy and solid-looking – although the typical Regency chair with sabre legs, based on the *klismos* depicted on many Greek vases, is very graceful.

As in France, the rage was for Egyptian motifs, inspired by Napoleon's Egyptian campaigns. This influence was manifest in table supports in the shape of winged lions, monogods and sphinxes and in motifs such as palmettes, lion masks and paws, scarabs, obelisks and even crocodiles.

Two non-Classical styles – chinoiserie and Gothick – were to a lesser extent enjoying a popular revival at this time.

WALLS

PAINT The large plain surfaces were frequently painted a single colour and might then be decorated with a discreet repeat pattern, which could either be stencilled or painted freehand.

Very much a feature of the Regency style is the *faux* finish – a painted surface imitating marble, woodgrain, bronze or porphyry. This might be used on furniture as well as woodwork, fire surrounds and the like.

TEXTILES Walls might have fabric stretched over them – silk damask, lustring (glazed taffeta), tabouret (half-silk in a plain colour) or wool. Rooms sometimes had fabric draped from the ceiling, like a tent.

WINDOWS An abundance of drapery – sometimes elaborately looped and swagged and

heavy with fringes – decorated the tops of windows, usually over embroidered sub-curtains. Where several windows were grouped together along a wall, one continuous drapery would be festooned along the top. After 1819 fabrics were lighter and designs more fanciful – many of them printed. Flowered chintz was popular.

FLOORS

The same types of flooring were used as in the Georgian period. Carpet was even more fashionable than before: popular patterns included hexagons and florals. Brussels weave, woven like Wilton but with looped instead of cut pile, was a new innovation.

FURNITURE

Although mahogany was still popular, it is rosewood that typifies the Regency. Other woods

OPPOSITE FAR LEFT All the pictures on these two pages are from Plas Teg, a striking Jacobean stately home in North Wales. Here, a strong Regency feel is conveyed by George IV gilded chairs covered in satin and moiré and helped, of course, by the pedestal table and the striped brocade on the walls.

LEFT The beautiful lines of a classic Regency chaise longue set the scene in this sitting room. The carpet is a priceless Aubusson – a fragile and rare piece that not many people would wish to walk upon – but a less expensive later carpet would blend in well. Lighting is always a problem in a period interior, but here the appropriate soft glow has been achieved by wiring an alabaster urn with a simple bulb holder.

BELOW Regency and Empire interiors are typified by symmetry and Classical inspiration. This meticulously balanced arrangement makes good use of ornate candelabra.

used for veneers were maple and the more exotic zebra wood. Ormolu decoration was replaced by inlay and galleries in brass.

The sofa table, in front of a sofa, was intended to hold books, tea things and so on. Like the Pembroke table, it had flaps, but it was larger and the flaps were on the short ends instead of the long sides. Sheraton quartetto tables, in nests, came into fashion, as did combined work-and-games tables. Round pedestal tables (loo tables) were popular.

Sideboards with flanking pedestals topped by urns, in the style introduced by Adam, were still seen, but more common was the bow-fronted type developed by Hepplewhite and Sheraton.

The chiffonier, which could be used instead of a sideboard, was new. It was a pedestal cupboard with a shelf or shelves behind a pair of doors; these might be of solid wood or they might have centre panels filled with brass wire backed by silk.

On chairs with two or more backrails the top one was sometimes carved to resemble rope. Such "Trafalgar" chairs are said to have been a compliment to Nelson. A more informal lifestyle resulted in more comfortably upholstered chairs. Rooms, except for dining rooms, were arranged for conversation in groups.

LIGHTING

Wax candles continued to be widely used, and *torchères* were very fashionable. The new designs of oil lamp had a significant effect on daily life.

ACCESSORIES

Plant stands reflected the fashion for enjoying flowering plants indoors.

Over the fireplace, a large oblong mirror was preferred to a picture. Another popular style was the round mirror surmounted by an eagle.

TOP LEFT An ebonized Regency console table, complete with urns and candelabra, is surmounted by a massive gilt mirror.

TOP RIGHT A bedroom in Plas Teg, North Wales, which has exceptional marquetry panelling with inset mirrors. In front of the mirror stands a pair of Regency chairs and a games table.

BOTTOM LEFT Regency style is often seen as stiff and formal, but it does have its comfortable, lived-in side, as can be seen in the friendly clutter of this library.

BOTTOM RIGHT A Regency ebonized chair and table in a wonderfully warm setting created by marquetry panelling.

OPPOSITE Another view of the library shown in the picture above left reveals a sensational late 18thC desk and an incredible Egyptianesque chair. Both are slightly battered and distressed; nevertheless they demonstrate the superb workmanship and design of Regency furniture and the tremendous interest in all things Classical.

FAR LEFT TOP This small dining room in a terraced cottage in King's Road, London, has all the elements that one would expect to find in a Regency-style room: the typical convex mirror of the period, the side cabinet with a pair of cornucopia, the elegant table and chairs and the "marble" floor – effective even though made from vinyl sheeting.

FAR LEFT BOTTOM This was a period of opulence and grand style, so you should not be afraid to use interesting colours and extravagant drapes. Large Persian carpets on polished boards are more authentic than wall-to-wall Wilton. The fireplace in this room owes its dramatic effect to a marbled paint finish – marbling is not difficult, it just requires patience and a good book on the subject. The porcelain on the tea table is authentic early and mid-19thC, which can still be found quite inexpensively in job lots in country sale rooms.

LEFT Regency style comes into its own in large, grand spaces. The strong lines so typical of Regency furniture are particularly suited to rooms that boast high, decorated ceilings, impressive columns and intricate mouldings. This grand dining area, once a hallway, is notable for its symmetrical arrangement of superb elements – an original double pedestal dining table and chairs (with two carvers), a niche displaying fine porcelain and intricate wallpaper whose stripes emphasize the room's proportions.

BELOW A formal Regency setting is here given a leafy, country feeling chiefly by the choice of wall colour and curtain fabric. This room has a Classical Georgian symmetry about it, an effective a foil for the beautiful chairs which are perfect examples of their type, with their exuberant scrolling arms and wide sabre legs in the characteristic style.

TOP This room in Parham House in West Sussex was given its present cream and gold decoration at the end of the 18thC. The marble relief on the fireplace, the French Empire clock in a partly bronzed ormolu case and the reflected pillars all show the period's fascination with Classicism.

ABOVE A Regency mood can be created by judicious use of black paired with either gold or yellow. The period also saw the introduction of many fine mirrors, either in the form shown here or the very typical convex mirror with gilt frame, adorned with an eagle or other decorative theme.

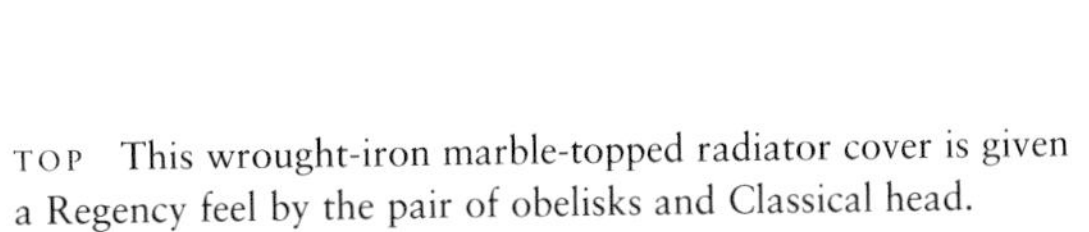

TOP This wrought-iron marble-topped radiator cover is given a Regency feel by the pair of obelisks and Classical head.

ABOVE These marvellous black and gilt Regency chairs set the scene in a hallway with *faux marbre* blocks on the wall and an imitation black and white marble floor.

LEFT An unusual painted marble wall finish provides a strong background to this exuberant William IV side table, with a collection of marble and a bronze bust.

TOP A good Regency card or tea table and a pair of dining chairs, c.1820, are augmented with a wonderful, exuberant display of white lilies.

ABOVE A collection of 19thC treen (turned wooden items) sits on a Regency tea table, making an evocative composition.

Empire

The French Empire style which arose in France in the 1790s has been described as Napoleon's propaganda vehicle. Fashionable throughout Europe, the style is typified by interiors luxuriously draped with brilliant-coloured silk, rather like grand military tents, and furnished with rather massive plain-shaped pieces of furniture generously decorated with ormolu and gilt.

In France, as in England, this was a Classical period. There are, however, other strong influences on Empire style. A note of antique grandeur was overlaid with motifs celebrating Napoleon's military prowess and Egyptian motifs in particular became important after his campaigns in Egypt. Decorations included the sphinx and winged lion, Greek caryatids, the swan (Josephine's emblem was the black swan) and the Imperial eagle. Other popular motifs include stars, palmettes, lotus flowers, medallions, trophies of arms and the Napoleonic bee.

WALLS

FABRIC Walls were frequently hung with plain or simply patterned silk; popular colours were bright yellow, brilliant green and crimson. Fabric was sometimes pleated onto the walls but usually was draped in a tent-like fashion. The join between walls and tented ceiling might be covered with a pennant-shaped pelmet.

WALLPAPER France made the best wallpapers at this time, often designed to imitate fabric. Designs to match curtaining and upholstery fabric were quite usual. Strips of paper, made to look like furnishing borders, were often pasted around the room.

Scenic papers, showing views of cities – Paris, London, Constantinople – and illustrations from literature, were very fashionable.

Dados and chair rails were usual, although in tented rooms they would be hidden by swathes of fabric.

WINDOWS

Pull-up curtains were not fashionable at this time. Instead, pairs of curtains, often muslin, would be topped with elaborately swathed, silk draperies, fixed permanently in position. Sometimes a plain blind matching the silk drapery could be pulled down behind.

FURNITURE

Furniture shapes were basically simple and geometric, usually adapted from antique designs, often incorporating a sphinx, Josephine's swan, a winged lion or caryatid. The Napoleonic Wars made it difficult to obtain exotic rosewood and mahogany; instead, furniture makers used native woods such as burr maple, beech and walnut.

Sabre legs were used on many chairs, and there were stools based on the Roman folding stool. The use of animal forms for furniture legs, borrowed from Ancient Egypt, was common on console tables, gueridons (circular candlestands on a plinth) and so on. Day-beds might be single-ended chaises longues or have high backs in subtly varying styles.

LIGHTING

The new oil lamps were a flexible and efficient form of lighting, but wax candles were still preferred in elegant society, especially for grand occasions.

ACCESSORIES

The Sèvres factory had developed a formula for hard-paste porcelain. This was decorated with rich colours, often with touches of gold; sometimes pieces had blobs of enamel to represent gems. Shapes were based on Greek, Roman and Egyptian precedents or on cylinders and spheres.

The finest metalwork was by Pierre-Philippe Thomire. He made bronze mounts for fine furniture, clock cases for Sèvres, large urns delicately modelled with foliage and figures, and candelabra.

OPPOSITE This room in a flat in central London has a strong French and Swedish Empire feel to it – styles closely linked to the English Regency look but with their own peculiarities. The sofa is Swedish, c.1810. The armchairs from the same period are French: they are inlaid with gilt decoration and are covered in a French silk fabric with a very formal air. The curtain fabric is a design called the "Napoleonic Bee" which is still available in ivory, green, red and bright blue. The commode on the right is French, c.1810, as is the chandelier.

BELOW LEFT These classic Regency black and gilt pieces give a modern bathroom an early 19thC flavour. It is not advisable to place an antique too close to a working radiator – firstly it diminishes the amount of heat produced and secondly it could seriously damage the piece.

BELOW RIGHT Exquisite black and gilt Regency pieces such as these, with their fine delicate lines, bring a sense of period to a more modern setting of a marbled wall with *faux bois* skirting.

OPPOSITE AND RIGHT Here and on the next few pages we see the epitome of the American Empire style in Richard Jenrette's house on the Hudson River in New York State. Every effort has been made to recreate this exceptional house as it once was, replacing all the original pieces of furniture: this has involved Mr Jenrette in years of research and travel to other continents. All the furniture is American and was made between 1800 and 1820, much of it for the Livingstone family who once owned the property. The sense of perfect Classical proportion is everywhere in the room shown on the right, accentuated by urns and busts. The octagonal study shown opposite has walls that have been painted to resemble stone and a strongly patterned carpet, specially designed to recapture the opulent lines of the period.

American Empire

The American version of the Empire style succeeded the lighter and more delicate Neo-classical interiors of the Federal period after about 1810. Gradually American Empire developed into the Greek Revival style, which flourished from about 1820 to 1840.

The shift toward greater opulence came first with furniture. The delicate lines inspired by Hepplewhite and early Sheraton designs were replaced by more massive shapes. Pieces were often ornately carved and decorated with gilt, brass inlay and ormolu.

As in Europe, ancient styles and decorative motifs – Greek, Roman and Egyptian – were taken as models and inspiration, but American designs stopped short of the extremes of elaboration sometimes found in Europe.

Early furniture was richly decorated with carving, gilt and ormolu. Later, less expensive painted or stencilled decoration became fashionable. In the last part of the period the rich carving and elaborate decoration disappeared, large expanses of beautifully figured mahogany or rosewood being considered decorative enough in themselves.

Two rooms in the Metropolitan Museum of Art's American Wing illustrate the early Empire and later Greek Revival styles.

The first room is set up for a card party. Decoration and furnishing are altogether richer and more imposing than in previous periods: the materials are mahogany, marble, electric-blue Chinese silk, gilt, ormolu and crystal glass. The mahogany chair and sofa shapes are based on the Roman *currule* stool with its X-shaped base; a pier table in rosewood, mahogany and marble has gilt swan supports terminating in dolphin feet at the front; and the card table is inlaid with various woods (including rosewood) and with brass, and has carved and gilded supports, the front one taking the form of a winged female figure in a proud, heroic posture.

To add to the richness of the room, the upholstery fabric is glowing blue silk and the woodwork, including the cornice, is in mahogany. The Classical

theme is continued with a marble fireplace, doorcase and window surround topped by a frieze and an Aubusson carpet with a design of hexagons and stylized flowers. Not in the least Classical, however, is the French scenic wallpaper, of a type very popular in the Federal period.

The second room represents a parlour of around 1835 and the whole decoration is in typical Greek Revival style. Plain plastered walls painted a creamy beige are offset by white Ionic columns, pilasters, doorcase, deep cornice and woodwork. The Brussels carpet completely covering the floor is a glowing dark red with a design in shades of gold. The parlour suite that furnishes the room is upholstered in red rep decorated with a gold centre medallion and border. All the furniture is of mahogany and in the late style; its broad simple curves are unadorned by carving or by ormolu. On the round table is the simplest and most discreet gilt decoration.

Lighting was more efficient by this period: the room contains a tall table oil lamp and a pair of double-branch Argand lamps. Both are Classically inspired, the first with a column base, the second with oil reservoirs in the shape of Greek amphorae.

ABOVE LEFT This upstairs landing in Richard Jenrette's house (see page 131) makes a perfect setting for a New York bookcase and an octagon table and chairs – all American pieces made between 1800 and 1820. The owner has ensured historical accuracy in every detail, down to the carpet runner on the stairs and the Persian rug on polished boards on the landing.

LEFT The early years of the 19thC are a particularly interesting period in the development of the American domestic interior, encompassing as they do American Empire, American Classical and late Federal styles. Many of these influences are apparent in Richard Jenrette's house. In this hallway, as elsewhere in the house, he has achieved a wonderful feeling of unity – all the elements mesh together. The generous sweep of the staircase is emphasized by the deep green carpet and the decorative stair rods. The inlaid wooden floor is copied from a floor in the Tsar's Palace in St Petersburg.

OPPOSITE The stark white architraves and marble skirtings here are distinctly Classical, and lead the eye into the drawing room with its strongly patterned carpet. The mirrors are both excellent examples of early 19thC craftsmanship – the pier tables with mirrored bases are called "petticoat tables" because the ladies would check their hemlines before going out to make sure that not a hint of ankle was showing. Lilies are the perfect flower for this style of interior.

OPPOSITE This is the dining room of Richard Jenrette's house. The furniture for this room was made mainly in New York. The chairs are by Duncan Phyfe, probably the most famous of all American furniture makers: he worked in New York producing designs based on Sheraton, English Regency and French Empire styles. The room has a Classical symmetry accentuated by the painted panels and arrangement of the pictures.

ABOVE LEFT In the drawing room is an exceptional collection of Duncan Phyfe furniture re-upholstered in a fabric design called "Napoleonic Bee" – a French Empire pattern which is still being made today. Over the fireplace is a painting of George Washington, and the mantelpiece boasts a Washington clock.

ABOVE RIGHT Marbled walls make a perfect backdrop to beautiful late Federal furniture, characterized by its delicate lines and inlay work.

TOP Alongside the formal Colonial styles of the early 19thC, a country version developed. Here, simple polished boards and white walls with strong matt colours on skirtings, architraves and doors make for a more relaxed way of life. The patchwork quilt partially covers an early 19thC day-bed. The simple but effective drapes add a touch of colour and style.

MIDDLE A lovely country Colonial bedroom has as its centrepiece a good 19thC bed with its original quilt. At the window, summer drapes of unlined muslin make the most of light and air. The simple Queen Anne maple side chair is from an earlier date, c.1760–90.

BOTTOM This Empire work table shows how the refined lines of Sheraton developed into more massive forms. The natural figuring of mahogany was by this stage considered decoration enough. Note how the below-dado panelling, the skirting, the fireplace, the architraves and the door are painted a single strong matt colour to contrast with the white wall above.

OPPOSITE This guest bedroom in Richard Jenrette's house is decorated in its original colour scheme of deep mauve and yellow. This unusual combination sets off the fine Federal bed, Empire chest and the églomisé mirror typically surmounted by an eagle.

FAR LEFT TOP This hallway in a Park Avenue apartment in New York is given a dramatic Empire feel by the painted stone effect on the walls, the mahogany door with gilt detailing, the pair of early 19thC hall chairs, the Classically inspired painted floor and, of course, the alert pose of Filagree, the dalmation.

FAR LEFT BOTTOM AND NEAR LEFT This magnificent early 19thC American house in Connecticut has beautifully painted figured wood-effect panelling and black marble-effect skirting boards, which make a dramatic setting for a Biedermeier inlaid cupboard (Biedermeier is the name given to the German and Austrian variant of the late Empire style) and a pair of matching side chairs with typical ebonized back splats. In front of the Classical-style fireplace, two Empire sofas face one another.

ABOVE Glimpsed through the doorway here is an American Classical sofa dating from c.1835. Most of the elements are from approximately the same period, although they differ in stylistic influence. The sofa is flanked by a pair of Federal cherrywood candlestands, the lamp bases are Chinese export ware, the Regency pedestals in the hall are reproductions and the urn-shaped wooden containers on top of them are late 18thC English knife urns without tops.

TOP LEFT, TOP RIGHT AND BOTTOM LEFT All the photographs on these two pages are of Kenneth Hockin's tiny studio apartment in the Village, New York, which he has transformed into an Empire haven. The large chest (pictured top left) is really a transition piece between Empire, with its Ionic columns, and early Victorian. The mood is set by the obelisk, the Napoleonic prints and the Empire chair. In the top right picture, the wallscape of black and gilt has an unmistakable late American Empire feel. The American marble-topped console table by Joseph Meeks is laden with distinctly linear articles that accentuate the Empire theme – French Empire clock with obelisks, lamp and candlestand, flower vases and plant. The Regency convex mirror is given added style by a pair of tassels. The tub chair is William IV.

BOTTOM RIGHT The dining room of the apartment is actually the hallway. The melon yellow walls were inspired by an American Empire room-set in a museum. The old pine cupboard was found discarded in the street. The glassware is American flint glass. Notice how the subject matter of the painting above the cupboard has been echoed by a real still life, and how much more effective two small vases of sweetpeas are than one.

OPPOSITE This view of Kenneth Hockin's studio apartment shows how a single strong visual image – in this case a portrait of Napoleon – can set a period scene. Helped by the miniatures around it and the little bedside cabinet piled with boxes, it totally dominates the bright, modern sofa.

Creating the look

Colours Strong bright colours are typical of this style – brilliant green, yellow or crimson, offset with gold.

Walls A fairly simple treatment is appropriate, with large plain surfaces painted a single pale colour. You could add a border design, either painted freehand or stencilled, with a simple Greek or Egyptian motif.

Hanging fabric on the wall loosely to create the effect of a luxurious tent is an appropriate strategy. Pictorial wallpapers are a good choice for an Empire-style room. Or choose a design that imitates fabric – edged with braid, this would give a tented feel to the room.

Furniture The heavier, rather grand pieces of furniture are expensive. Fortunately, sabre-legged chairs, bow-fronted sideboards and drum tables are also typical of the time. Originals of these designs are more affordable, and good reproductions are available.

Day-beds are typical of this style; they were made in a wide variety of designs. Hang fabric from a corona above a double-ended day-bed to create a tent-like impression.

Lighting Oil lamps – as wall lights, pendants and table lamps – were available, so there is a wide choice of fittings to choose from. Rooms were more brightly lit but did not approach present-day levels of illumination; so keep background levels low and concentrate on creating pools of light.

Floors Large carpets in rich colours with rather stylized repeat motifs of laurel wreaths, hexagons and the circular designs known as paterae would suit a Regency or Empire room.

Soft furnishings Pairs of lightweight curtains in a simple muslin fabric are right for this period, but they should be topped with grand, elaborately looped swags decorated with a mass of imposing fringing. Behind the curtains you might like to have a plain roller blind made in the same fabric as the pelmet. Where there are several windows close together, continue the drapery across the whole series.

Damasks and plain silks are suitable, as are designs with stylized laurel wreaths, swans and the Napoleonic bee. Flowered chintz would also be a suitable choice for a late Regency room. However, avoid the strong contrast of "Regency stripes", as these are actually a fashion of the 1950s: much more in keeping are self-coloured fabrics woven with alternate matt and shiny stripes.

Ornaments Gilded mirrors sound the appropriate note. A rectangular mirror over a fireplace is authentic for the time. Ornaments in the shape of obelisks or sphinxes help to set the scene. Porcelain and pottery richly decorated with colour and gilding, but with rather severe Neo-classical shapes, suit this style.

Finishing touches A witty and much less expensive alternative to a large carpet is to paint a design directly onto smooth floorboards.

Suggested music: Beethoven's *Piano Concerto No. 5* ("Emperor") and *Violin Concerto*; Schubert's *Trout Quintet*.

Opposite This wonderful rich red in the music room of Richard Jenrette's house on the Hudson River is carefully matched to the original colour. This was certainly a period when no one was afraid of strong colours – it was a time of confidence and opulence, as we can see from the mirror, which once belonged to Madame Jumel of the Morris Jumel Mansion in New York. The window benches are reproductions of original benches now in the Brooklyn Museum. The carpet was designed to complement the wall colour and the gilding.

Above Another view of the opulent music room. The sensational early 19thC furniture has quite a history. It was purchased in 1823 by the Donaldson family and shipped from North Carolina. The boat sank and the furniture lay underwater for three months. When it was brought to the surface, the only damage was water stains on the fabric.

Victorian

Queen Victoria came to the British throne in 1837 and ruled until 1901. For the British middle classes, this was a time of extreme self-confidence: the self-made man was proud of his achievements and used his house as a vehicle to display the wealth gained by his industry. The family was paramount in the Victorian scale of values, and the home was important as a haven of comfort and family life.

ABOVE Colour and pattern have dominant roles in the Victorian interior. This glimpse of a hallway shows just how evocative a busy patterned wallpaper and colourwashed lincrusta below dado level can be. Prints in gilt frames and the obligatory barometer add further credibility.

RIGHT AND FAR RIGHT, TOP AND BOTTOM A set-piece of Victorian style, designed by Jonathan Hudson, which depends for its considerable impact on a rich variety of colours, fabrics, plants and pictures. The mix of old and new fabrics works particularly well. The exuberant drapes have tremendous style and are typical of the age. The design of this room was based on the Linley Sambourne house, an authentic late Victorian villa in Stafford Terrace, London. The corner of the room pictured far top right shows the Victorian obsession with detail – the lacy lampshade, the fabric on the mantelpiece, the firescreen, the chair cover – all are absolutely authentic. Victorians had a basic aversion to light and air and were keen to bring greenery indoors where they could appreciate it in comfort. In the far bottom right picture an excess of flowering plants cascade from a converted Victorian cellaret (wine cooler), and on the mantelpiece a credenza overflows with love-lies-bleeding (*Amaranthus caudatus*).

OPPOSITE All the pictures on these two pages are of a house designed by Christophe Gollut. This drawing room has the womb-like atmosphere favoured by the Victorians. The first impression is of colour – from the aubergine cotton fabric on the walls to the terracotta marble paint finish on the cornice.

LEFT The attractive paint finish is shown to best advantage on the architraves and skirting boards.

RIGHT TOP AND BOTTOM The Victorians were inveterate travellers and collectors of curios. The French Empire marble-topped commode (right) sports a collection of the kind one would expect of a Victorian gentleman. Over the Louis XV sofa (below right), draped with oriental and European fabrics, hangs an oil painting depicting a procession in Ceylon.

The Victorian townhouse, to 1870

Eclecticism is a keynote of Victorian townhouse interiors. A number of different historical styles were popular simultaneously. Elizabethan and Gothic appealed to the Victorian sense of continuity with tradition, satisfying a deep sense of nostalgia. Even styles that were not truly indigenous, such as Rococo (Louis XV), enjoyed popularity.

Mid-Victorian rooms were usually full of pattern in rich colours on carpet, walls and curtains. Walls would be divided into dado, infill and frieze, with perhaps a painted embossed paper on the dado and a patterned one above; the woodwork might be varnished a dark colour or grained. Windows were heavily draped and usually had lace curtains or blinds as well, making the rooms dark during the day. There was drapery everywhere; even the mantelpiece would be festooned with fabric.

A typical room of the period would be crammed full of furniture, much of it with luxuriously thick, well-sprung and deeply buttoned upholstery. It was not considered necessary for furniture to be matched in suites. As well as an assortment of sofas and armchairs, there were any number of occasional chairs. Any space left over would be filled up with small tables and, of course, a whatnot or two.

RIGHT Kelims, cushions, collections and yet more collections can give a Victorian feel to any room. The copper lustreware on the mantelpiece was a particular favourite of the period.

OPPOSITE TOP LEFT A kelim covers a Victorian chesterfield laden with cushions made from pieces of tapestry and carpet. Leather-bound books are piled nonchalantly around the room. Blue-and-white porcelain and stoneware complete the collection.

OPPOSITE TOP RIGHT Here the seating is modern, the oils and watercolours not all Victorian, but the sense of period is nonetheless evoked with the eclectic mix of fabrics, the clutter of frames on the side tables and the tight grouping of paintings.

OPPOSITE BOTTOM LEFT A fresh look at Victorian style from the decorator Jane Churchill who has created a pleasing symmetry. The round tables can be bought at very little expense – many of them are just made of chipboard – but they do require good heavy fabric covers, interlined and often weighted down.

OPPOSITE BOTTOM RIGHT The Victorians had certainly never heard of the dictum "Less is more". No surface was left bare. Here, a massing of oils, watercolours and miniatures, all in good frames, proves that the whole is greater than the parts.

Pictures and miniatures covered the walls, and every available surface would be crammed with trophies, souvenirs, lamps, vases, pottery figures, shell-covered boxes, needlework items, domed glass cases containing waxed flowers and bric-à-brac of all sorts. No home would have been complete without a selection of the leafy green plants so beloved of the Victorians – ferns, trailing plants and aspidistras.

WALLS

Although, early on, colour schemes were light with warm sunny colours (except for the library and the dining room, where red flock was the fashionable thing), soon a preference for strong, rather gaudy colours became apparent. The fashion for dividing the wall into dado, infill and frieze came in strongly from about 1860.

WALLPAPER Mass-produced from the 1840s, wallpaper was available in a wide range of qualities. Hand-printed papers were also produced but these were expensive. There was a wide range of patterns. In the 1860s white-and-gold designs became popular for drawing rooms furnished in the "Louis" styles (see page 98). A.W.N. Pugin, decorator of the Houses of Parliament, designed a number of papers with medieval motifs – stylized roses, fleur-de-lys, pineapples, geometric trellis – which suited Gothic interiors. Repeat patterns of flowers were fashionable, as were embossed papers used on both ceilings and walls and then painted over. William Morris and Co. started producing their famous wallpapers in the 1860s.

PAINT Walls might be painted with coloured distemper. A room treated in this way might have a border of a repeat pattern which might be either stencilled or painted freehand.

WOODWORK This might be painted or grained and in Gothic interiors would frequently be dark-stained.

WINDOWS

Heavy curtains helped to prevent carpets and upholstery from fading. The fashionable fabrics of the early 1860s are listed in *Cassell's Household Guide* as "all kinds of damask, moreen, and rep ..." as well as a new fabric from France called Timbuctoo, which was "... striped horizontally in white, scarlet, black and yellow on a green, red or blue ground".

Draped pelmets were still fashionable in the early part of the period. Later on, an ornate type of flat pelmet, called a lambrequin, was popular: this had a shaped outline and extended some way down the sides of the curtains. Curtains were often hung on heavy brass poles.

Lace or muslin undercurtains were used next to the glass to keep dust and dirt out of the room. Roller blinds were quite common also and were often decorative; some "transparent" blinds were painted with designs of landscapes and other subjects.

The mantelpiece often had its own curtain to match the other soft furnishings. This took the form of a board covered with fabric with a flounce of material hanging down.

OPPOSITE This room, designed by Jonathan Hudson, was inspired by an exceptional collection of Victorian paintings, many of them by Sir Lawrence Alma-Tadema whose work was popular around 1870–90. The strong wall colours, the soft pools of light, the indoor palms and the interesting mix of furniture styles are typical of this late Victorian period.

LEFT Not all Victorian interiors were dark and cluttered. Here, a simple Victorian chest, blue sponge-effect wallpaper, an armchair covered in white calico and a small oriental rug conjure up the plainer aspects of Victorian decoration. The blue Nailsea glass flasks were greatly admired at the time and work well when flanked by metallic lamps.

FLOORS

Carpets with large patterns were popular, and it was fashionable for the border of floorboards left around the edges of the room to be stained, painted or perhaps marbled – or sometimes covered with felt. In a grand house the border might be of parquet. A canvas drugget was sometimes placed on top of the carpet to protect it from wear. Floorcloth, often elaborately patterned, was an economical form of floor covering.

LIGHTING

Oil table lamps were still a commonplace form of lighting until they were superseded by gas in the 1870s. Candles no longer played a major part in the lighting of interiors.

FURNITURE

Mahogany was the most popular Victorian wood. Later on, there was a vogue for walnut and satinwood.

Heavily carved, and often artificially blackened, oak was used for "Elizabethan" and "Gothic" pieces; craftsmen sometimes complained that pieces had to be "... stained to imitate old, and sold for old". In addition antique furniture was often cannibalized to make new pieces. It was usually the ornament rather than the shape that distinguished a piece of Victorian Gothic furniture.

A material, little used before, that became very fashionable in the middle of the century was papier mâché. This was usually lacquered black and decorated with mother-of-pearl or "paste" inlay and/or painted flowers and fruit. A whole variety of charming small pieces was made – chairs, work boxes, trays, bedheads, small tables and the like. The best-known makers were Jennens and Bettridge of Birmingham.

Brass bedsteads were a Victorian innovation; the grander ones frequently had a half-tester construction.

The dining room was important both for eating and for family prayer gatherings. The sideboard was a massive affair, often surmounted by a large mirror. Although some shapes were quite simple, with fairly restrained ornament, there was a fashion for heavily carved pieces. Two exhibited at the International Exhibition of 1862 were the "Shakespeare" and "Robinson Crusoe" sideboards by Thomas Tweedy and his pupil Gerrard Robinson. Both are very detailed pieces; the former is covered with scenes and figures from many of Shakespeare's plays, the latter with incidents from Defoe's tale of the island castaway.

A dining table was usually rectangular, with square or rounded ends. It was solid in construction, with four bulbous turned legs, and could be extended with additional leaves. Tablecloths were used at mealtimes, and between meals the dining table would be covered with a baize, linen or velvet cloth. Although dining chairs – as well as tables, sideboards and so on – might be in Elizabethan or Gothic styles, the balloon-back shape was the most popular. It went out of fashion around 1870, although manufacture continued. Balloon-back dining room chairs had straight legs. The same style of chair was also made for the drawing room, but with cabriole legs from the 1850s.

Davenport desks were popular – small writing desks, usually with drawers at the side. Chiffoniers and oval or round tilt-top pedestal (or loo) tables were a feature of morning rooms in early and mid-Victorian upper-class houses, and of drawing rooms in middle-class ones. No home was complete without its whatnot – a piece of furniture with shelves for the display of knick-knacks, an essential item in the Victorian household.

An important piece of hall furniture was the stand to take coats, hats and umbrellas. This sometimes incorporated a seat; alternatively, it might include a table, though sometimes there would be a separate, narrow table for visitors' calling cards. An oak or mahogany longcase clock was a typical hallway feature also, and there was usually a hall chair. Some hall furniture was made of cast iron.

ABOVE Among numerous specialist paint effects employed in this 19thC Victorian Gothic hallway are a *faux* stone finish on the chimneypiece, *faux* limewash on the walls, woodgraining on the panelled door, and a *trompe l'oeil* cornice between the tops of the walls and the ceiling. The oriental carpet, laid over parquet flooring, is equally appropriate to the period and the style.

OPPOSITE TOP Like the deep-buttoned upholstered, balloon-back chairs, and the predominantly red and yellow colour scheme, the gilt-framed painting over the chimneypiece and the displays of decorative artefacts on the mantelshelf and in the built-in shelves are typical of a mid-19thC Victorian parlour.

OPPOSITE BOTTOM LEFT A good-quality Eastlake-style fireplace provides the focal point in the library of a late 19thC American Victorian house.

OPPOSITE BOTTOM CENTRE As in many 19thC American Victorian parlours, a "swan rocker" chair (of c.1850) stands in front of a marble chimneypiece at the Old Merchant's House, in New York.

OPPOSITE BOTTOM RIGHT The marble fireplace in the parlour of Cedar Grove, in Vicksburg, Mississippi, USA, was imported from Italy and dates to the 1840s – the decade in which the house was built. The paraffin (kerosene) lamps on the mantelshelf are early 19thC French Empire style. The pair of upholstered chairs are American Victorian and feature "Southern style" turned front and upper-back legs.

By the 1830s springs for seat furniture were in general production in Birmingham, making possible the typically Victorian opulent, rounded shapes. Deep buttoning which accentuated the thickness and curvaceousness of the upholstery was very popular. Upholstered pieces included the circular or rectangular ottoman around which several people could sit, the chaise longue, various types of sofa and novelty pieces such as the sociable (an S-shaped couch allowing the two occupants to face each other) or the *tête-à-tête* (rather like two armchairs joined by a single long seat with a small table fixed in the middle). Early in the period, chairs and sofas completely covered with upholstery were in vogue; later on, styles with exposed frames of polished mahogany or rosewood became popular.

There were innumerable kinds of occasional chair – typical are the spoon-back and the prie-dieu. The latter, with its low seat and tall T-shaped back, looks rather strange until you realize that instead of sitting on it you were intended to kneel on the seat and lean with your elbows on the upholstered top rail.

Accessories

Advances in mass production made silverware cheaper. Electroplating superseded Sheffield Plate: the process required less silver and worn articles could be easily re-plated.

Major Victorian developments in porcelain include Minton's *pâte sur pâte* (in white relief on a dark background) and the creamy-white, marble-like parian ware introduced by Copeland and widely used for figurines, often of Classical subjects. Coalport favoured a Neo-rococo style. Large quantities of blue-and-white printed wares were made in Britain in imitation of Chinese export designs – these were far more ornate than Chinese taste would allow in wares for home consumption. Such pieces were cranked out by the thousands for the American and home markets.

Staffordshire pottery figures, whose naive charm is highly appealing, were made from around 1835 to 1895. Majolica pottery, with colourful glazes, was also popular. It was made, most notably, by Minton.

Late Victorian

By the last quarter of the 19th century there was also a nostalgic look back to the time of Queen Anne. A relaxed informality was the keynote of this style. Rooms with inglenooks and "cosy corners" were furnished with antiques, though these were not necessarily of the Queen Anne period. A well-worn look was considered an advantage in such interiors. The Queen Anne style was in harmony with the rather bohemian mood of the Aesthetic Movement, on which it exerted a considerable influence.

An "Aesthetic" interior was less heavy, less eclectic and more casual than rooms in the mainstream Victorian tradition. There was an emphasis on asymmetry and on hand-crafted objects – mass production was considered "philistine", the antithesis of the Aesthetic Movement. In these rooms a lived-in look was a positive virtue: old pieces handed down from grandparents were mixed with Anglo-Japanese, often ebonized, rather angular furniture, and distinctive pieces made in bamboo.

Late Victorian also had a more formal side, giving rise to interiors decorated in a rather general "18th-century" style. These rooms were furnished with graceful, well-made reproduction pieces – typical styles were "after Chippendale" and so-called "Queen Anne" (actually in the style of Adam, Sheraton and Hepplewhite). Satinwood was the favourite wood.

LEFT TOP An opulent mid-19thC style has been created in this 1820s London house, lavishly decorated by Ian Lieber. The peach walls have been softened with a stipple, all the colours are muted and the magnificent mirror and elegant wall sconces all add to the light, glittering, regal style.

LEFT MIDDLE A carefully coordinated Victorian-style "designer" interior turns the wide bay window of this drawing room into a focal point with its extravagant use of chintz and thick tasselled fringing.

LEFT BOTTOM It is good to see a new breed of hotel paying close attention to period style. The Dorset Square Hotel in London is a good example. This well-coordinated room has an interesting stencilled cornice frieze from a Caroline Warrender stencil kit. The plain grey marble fireplace and overmantel mirror are warmed by the wall colour, the floral fabrics and the simple but effective drapes.

RIGHT TOP Feather-filled cushions line the window seat in this wonderfully relaxing corner of a bedroom in a house in Southport, Connecticut. The table behind the chaise longue is made of American cherrywood, c.1800, the table in the foreground is a reproduction and the chair, c.1835, originates from the New York State Senate in Albany.

RIGHT MIDDLE This strong Victorian drawing room has quite masculine overtones – although in fact it was designed by a woman. The colours, the drapes and the variety of fabrics give this rather stately room a warm and homely feeling.

RIGHT BOTTOM A mixture of fabrics, patterns and rich strong colours give this room a cosy, Victorian feeling. Note how the proportions of the room are affected by the change of colour on the walls at dado height.

OPPOSITE This is a wonderful example of a Victorian interior that is neither dark nor overbearing. The house belongs to Linda Gumb, a dealer in antique fabrics and furniture, and her drawing room houses some excellent examples of her wares. The magnificent chandelier is made of Venetian glass: there was a time when this could be picked up for a song – but alas, those day are long gone.

OPPOSITE This grand Victorian mansion owned by Michael Wells could have been furnished by a wealthy Victorian collector. The 18thC marble bust sits happily with an 18thC French chair alongside a Victorian side table and celleret. The terracotta figures pick up the warm colour of the walls.

ABOVE This is another view of the same dining room. The chairs are 19thC English oak Gothick style and the magnificent oil portrait that appears to be framed by the painted panel is by Lely.

ALL PICTURES An absolutely authentic Victorian kitchen/dining room, while visually appealing, would hardly be practical. The kitchens and eating areas on these two pages present a happy compromise: modern appliances fitted into painted units, stripped pine dressers groaning with collections of pottery, a wonderful brick floor, an overhead hanging rail (an idea borrowed from the professional kitchen), an Aga fitted against a wall and fitted cupboards painted to look like an old French provincial armoire. All these rooms show an obvious enthusiasm for food and its preparation, and for the plates, pots, bowls and platters used for its presentation.

RIGHT This is the New Orleans bedroom in the American Museum, Bath. The massive pieces of furniture are typical of the period – c.1850. They were adapted from the Louis XV style by a famous cabinetmaker called Prudent Mallard who moved from New York to New Orleans in the late 1830s. The heaviness of the carved mahogany half-tester is softened by delicate use of white muslin and lace. The wallpaper, with its strong, richly coloured design, is absolutely in period.

OPPOSITE TOP LEFT The designer Melissa Wyndham has used a wonderful strong chintz fabric on the walls, windows and bedhangings, giving this room a distinctly 19thC flavour. When using such a fabric, a strong edging colour adds impact.

OPPOSITE TOP CENTRE A magnificent, ornately carved, Victorian Gothic four-poster bed takes pride of place in this American bedroom. Such richness of ornament is further enhanced by the oriental rugs and the carved and painted Medieval-style chest at the foot of the bed.

OPPOSITE TOP RIGHT Clever use of fabric and some good Victorian furniture and pottery make for a stylish bedroom in the Dorset Square Hotel, London.

OPPOSITE MIDDLE LEFT This early American Victorian, mahogany four-poster bed is dressed with heavily ruched and swagged floral-pattern hangings. As was often the case during the early to mid-19thC, these are coordinated ("en suite") with the window drapes.

OPPOSITE MIDDLE CENTRE This 18thC bed has been extravagantly but simply draped with a plain blue fabric – leaving a glimpse of an early crewelwork hanging behind. A treatment such as this requires nothing more than a bold touch and lots of fabric.

OPPOSITE MIDDLE RIGHT A truly theatrical bedroom in a New York State home, where the owner has taken out the ceiling and gone up into the roof space, making a minstrel gallery under the eaves. Hand-painted fabric decorates the walls, and the bold use of colours, plants and patterns turns this room into a dramatic stage-set.

OPPOSITE BOTTOM LEFT The heavily carved furniture in a bedroom at the Garth Woodside Mansion, in Hannibal, Missouri, is typical of grander American Victorian bedrooms. The bed is a rosewood and walnut half-tester, embellished with a broken pediment (on the headboard), turned finials and scrolling foliage motifs (also on the chair) derived from the Classical vocabulary of ornament.

OPPOSITE BOTTOM CENTRE Another bedroom in the American Victorian house shown *top centre* is dominated by a Renaissance-style four-poster bed. In keeping with late 19thC fashion, the heaviness of the carved and turned oak hardwood is alleviated by the matching pale and delicately patterned canopy, drapes, cushion covers and bedspread.

OPPOSITE BOTTOM RIGHT The striking deep mauve and yellow colour scheme in this bedroom is typical of the American Empire style that became fashionable during the 1820s and endured until around the middle of the 19thC. Other characteristic elements include an *églomisé* wall-mirror, surmounted by an eagle, a bow-fronted, mahogany chest of drawers, and a late Federal-style, four-poster bed with a pleated canopy – the latter gathered around a central rosette and edged with a swagged valance.

TOP LEFT This light airy room shows how effective antique white linen – tablecloths and old sheets – can be when used as bedspreads and curtains. The lace contrasts well against stark mahogany furniture. Nothing matches exactly – for example, one pelmet is of satin ribbons and the other is a piece of tasselled, embroidered fabric. The painted effects on the wall, and particularly the painted cherubs, give the room a romantic, feminine feel, accentuated by the heart-shaped chair-back and echoed by the dried flower wreath above the white-painted wrought-iron bed. A very sentimental, very Victorian room.

TOP RIGHT A light Victorian bedroom with a country feel in which diaphanous white muslin creates a Neo-medieval canopy.

MIDDLE LEFT This bedroom with its gleaming brass bed and restful colours has been thoughtfully designed. The curtains are of machine-made lace over cotton – very effective and simple. The patchwork quilt ties in with the cotton rug, and the floorboards have been colourwashed and sanded back to let the wood grain show through.

MIDDLE RIGHT This bedroom, feminine in mood, was designed by Jane Churchill. The features which make up this particular Victorian "designer" style are the complex pelmet design and flowing drapes, the old lace used under a glass top on the dressing table, and the coordinating bed-cover. The trompe l'oeil panels add a delicate dimension to the same wall.

BOTTOM LEFT Brass beds and, as here, painted cast-iron beds with contrasting brass detailing, became very fashionable during the last quarter of the 19thC. Better suited to the lighter colour schemes that came into vogue towards the end of the century, they were often dressed with white or off-white linen and machine- or handmade lace.

BOTTOM RIGHT The centrepiece of this very feminine bedroom is an 18thC bed – many pieces of this kind are now reproduced by companies such as Heritage of Petworth, West Sussex. Here the fabric has been kept soft and light, and the colour of the room decided by the 19thC patchwork quilt. Many of the other drapes are actually old linen, tablecloths and sheets which have intricate embroidery: these can be found in many country auction rooms and specialist shops.

TOP LEFT AND RIGHT Two interesting ways to give a dressing table a 19thC feel. The first is a good stripped-pine piece cluttered with the little collections so beloved of Victorian ladies. The second uses drapes to disguise practical storage space while allowing ample space on top for silver boxes, brushes and glass lustres converted into lamps.

MIDDLE LEFT This tiny 17thC bedroom is filled with a profusion of knick-knacks which give a cluttered, cosy Victorian feel. The table in the foreground holds a collection of fairings: these highly collectable small pottery groups were sold as souvenirs at resorts and fairgrounds from c.1860 to c.1914. The earliest fairing came from Saxony.

MIDDLE RIGHT This appealing child's room has a sweet, light simplicity. The bedspreads are made from tablecloths. In the hallway note the Lloyd loom chair which has been painted – these can still be acquired inexpensively – and a plain modern table completely covered in a patchwork quilt.

BOTTOM LEFT The main feature of one of the bedrooms at the Belle of the Bend inn, in Vicksburg, Mississippi, USA, is a Renaissance Revival half-tester bed, dated to c.1875. The light and airy ambiance of the room – fashionable in later 19thC American bedrooms – is established by the combination of off-whites and pale blues and pinks in the paintwork, the wallpaper and the soft furnishings.

BOTTOM RIGHT Cast- and wrought-iron bedsteads became increasingly fashionable on both sides of the Atlantic during the last quarter of the 19thC. Much of their popularity can be attributed to designers and style commentators of the period, who considered them far more "hygienic" than heavily draped four-poster beds, which inhibited the circulation of fresh air and were felt to be "dust traps" and breeding grounds for insect infestation.

FAR LEFT A turn-of-the-19thC enamelled bath-and-shower unit, on lion's paw feet.

LEFT Modern French bathroom fittings such as this double washbasin offer a 19thC look.

ABOVE A well-designed small bathroom built around an original Victorian vanity unit.

FAR LEFT Reproduction late 19thC tiles instantly establish the Victorian style.

LEFT A Victorian Gothic look is created by arched cornices and pelmets.

BELOW Modern reproductions of late 19thC and early 20thC painted toilets and washbasins are now widely available.

ABOVE An enamelled, roll-top Victorian bath, and a ceramic pedestal basin, underpin the rather spartan Victorian style of this attic bathroom.

BELOW Descending from an oculus in the ceiling, a late 19thC, white-painted, cast-iron spiral staircase provides a romantic link between this light and airy Victorian-style bathroom and its en-suite bedroom above.

RIGHT The original Victorian stained glass windows dictated the colour scheme in Christophe Gollut's London apartment. The walls are painted with green *faux* onyx panels; the bath-surround lined with slabs of black and gold Portoro marble.

OPPOSITE AND ABOVE This interior exudes American Gothic and contains many delightful surprises, all collected by Lee Anderson. Most of the pieces in Lee's collection are by the master craftsmen of this period. The rooms are dark but not oppressive. Every detail is perfect – from the candlesticks and cornices to the chairs and cushions. Tiffany may seem an odd bedfellow to the earlier Gothic pieces but his designs are so derivative that his work has been called "the last expression of the American Gothic".

ABOVE RIGHT, TOP AND BOTTOM Gothic as a style has a strong identity which transcends both period and country. In the top right picture note the 19thC Gothic standing cupboard, the modern copy of an Italian frame chair and the painting in Gothic taste – all elements in total harmony with the Stuart Interiors pomegranate pattern fabric. The bottom right picture shows a Strawberry Hill Gothick Windsor chair, c.1780, framed by a medieval stone arch and backed by a wool and linen pomegranate pattern which is based on a 17thC fabric. The iron candlestand was made by Stuart Interiors to a medieval design.

OVERLEAF, PAGE 168 In Lee Anderson's dining room in his New York Village home, the chairs and couch were made by Roux, the sideboard by Meeks in the 1830s, the table by A.J. Davis and the chairs by Crawford Riddell in Philadelphia in 1836. The lamps are by Tiffany. The whole effect depends upon the profusion of antiques from this period – some of high design, others mass-produced. In the top right picture we see exactly why Tiffany is often referred to in the same breath as American Gothic. The lamp seems to grow quite naturally from the table, which was probably made by Roux in New York c.1850. This table with its marble top and bronze heads and hooves shows the quality and integrity of design at this period. The bottom left picture is the story of three chairs. The exquisitely carved example in the foreground was made by Joseph Meeks, c.1850, the chair by the door was by A.J. Davis for Itarrick Castle (note the wonderful deer feet, shown up on the light-coloured flooring) and the chair in the hallway is by Boudine, New York, c.1855. We are reminded by the bottom right picture that the American Gothic Revival was very much a Victorian phenomenon. This combination of paintings, glassware and furniture from the 1830s and 40s has an unmistakable Victorian stamp upon it.

OPPOSITE A perfect American Gothic interior, again in Lee Anderson's home in New York's Village. The table on the right in a restrained taste which marks the transition from Classical to Gothic, the "hatbox" wallpaper (c.1820–30), the massive Gothic mirror by Roux, the collection of Gothic chairs – everything picks up the theme. The collection of parian figures (parian is an opaque white porcelain much loved by the Victorians), the sculpture and the small pieces of Gothic-influenced porcelain all blend in perfectly. (For captions to the pictures shown on this page, see page 167).

Creating the look

This is a style from which you can take as much or as little as you wish. If you find the rather heavy, dark colours of a mid-Victorian room too oppressive, choose the lighter ones appropriate for the early period. You may not want a complete interior in this style and, if this is the case, you could simply put together a Victorian corner in a room that does not otherwise evoke a specific period.

Colours Dark, rich reds, greens, blues and browns are appropriate for a Victorian interior. Patterns can also play an important role: if you are brave enough, try mixing various patterns in busy profusion.

Walls Walls divided into dado, infill and frieze will carry the authentic stamp of the period. You could choose an embossed paper for the dado, painted or varnished, with one of the many authentic Victorian wallpaper designs above. Alternatively, you could paint the walls and add a wallpaper or stencilled border. Woodwork could be grained or painted olive green.

Furniture Rounded, deep-buttoned shapes are the obvious choice for sofas and armchairs. Mahogany is the most characteristic wood of the era, and there are numerous Victorian chairs and tables still to be found; balloon-back chairs are particularly apt.

Soft furnishings Combine old or reproduction lace undercurtains with heavy velvet overcurtains and a draped and fringed pelmet. Match these up with a multi-layered round table with floor-length bottom cloth and one or more lace-edged cloths on top. As well as velvets and damasks, there is a whole range of suitable fabrics, from the ever-popular William Morris designs to distinctive Gothic patterns and rose-strewn printed cottons. Needlework of various sorts can be used for cushion covers, and for covering chair seats and stools. Sofas and large ottomans, upholstered with kelims, will give a room a Victorian flavour. Oriental rugs are ideal for this style of room, reflecting the Victorians' interest in exotic places. Paisleys, too, give an authentic touch.

Lighting There are many original gas lamps that have been converted in recent years to electricity. Reproduction Victorian lighting is also widely available. Take care how you fit the lighting, however, as all too often reproduction wall lights based on authentic gas fittings are installed upside-down: the ubiquitous flower-shaped shades would have had the opening facing the ceiling.

Flooring Large carpets in a traditional pattern, perhaps the red-and-blue "Turkey" design or a pattern of flowers and leaves, convey the right mood. Parquet makes a good border, as do dark-stained, painted or marbled boards. If you prefer a fitted carpet, the same type of traditional pattern or plain deep red, blue or green would work well. On top of a plain carpet you could place a flowery needlework rug.

Ornaments Staffordshire figures are perhaps the single most evocative type of Victorian ornament, but there are numerous other items that would help to build up the picture – for example, shell boxes, needlework pictures, waxed flowers under glass domes, family photographs and, of course, sentimental pictures of animals and children. Collections of such bric-à-brac and art, arranged on draped tables, whatnots, chiffoniers and windowsills, as well as on walls, will capture the flavour of the age.

Finishing touches An inexpensive feature can be created by making or buying a round chipboard table and covering it with a long, fringed cloth. Add one or more lace-edged cloths, a Paisley shawl or even an oriental rug, and arrange a collection of bric-à-brac on top.

Help the ambience along with, for example, Wagner's *Siegfried Idyll* on the hi-fi, or Elgar's *Chanson du Matin*.

Opposite This cosy parlour with its simple sprigged wallpaper is typical of an early Victorian country home. The mood is conveyed by a tapestry-covered chair, a kelim thrown over the table, plain floorboards with a highly decorative rug and a collection of Victorian Staffordshire figures – these, incidentally, are still relatively inexpensive, and even damaged pieces (which are even more easily affordable) can be used to great effect. A garland of garlic and herbs hung up to dry complete the ambience.

Above A simple, warm beige fabric edged in a complementary braid provides a perfect background to an Italian table, c.1860, and a pair of Victorian chairs. Flowers and candles provide an authentic finishing touch.

ALL PICTURES The Victorians were great travellers and collectors and an instant feeling of nostalgia for the age can be achieved in a house of any period by building a collection around a fireplace, a convenient corner or against a suitable wall. Here, a collection of treen and Mauchline ware crowd a whatnot beside a good Gothic chair (opposite top left). An interesting collection of luggage and sporting goods is randomly arranged in front of 15thC English carved panels (opposite top right). Fireplaces provide a good focal point for collections – for example, fine 18thC blue-and-white porcelain and 18thC English glassware (opposite bottom left). Choose a selection of coloured glass from the 18th and 19thC, an amusing collection of mantel dogs and a wall covered with prints framed in black (opposite bottom centre). Still more evocative is the wonderful inglenook covered with Victorian mugs, jugs, Toby jugs and teapots (opposite bottom right). Collections can certainly change the feel of a room: in the picture above, 19thC yellow-and-green majolica bring light and life to a 17thC interior. A collection of 18th, 19th and 20thC Chinese porcelain displayed on oriental boxes of different sizes gives an exotic feel to the hallway of Chilston Park, Kent (left). On the right, ivory inlaid tables and a coffer support exotic carvings, bronzes and a majolica jardinière.

OPPOSITE TOP LEFT Collections and individual pieces of interest can grace any kitchen wall. A pine spoon rack, hunting horn, 19thC spongeware and dried flowers have a warm, colourful, comfortable presence in this kitchen.

OPPOSITE TOP RIGHT This stencilled wallpaper is an excellent substitute for hand-painted stencilling and makes a perfect backdrop for the stencilled box, display of country flowers and late 19thC wooden toy.

OPPOSITE BOTTOM LEFT AND RIGHT This bathroom in a terraced house in Tunbridge Wells has a good Victorian country feel about it, thanks to the interesting wall colour and frieze and the plentiful use of fabric, from the kelim-covered ottoman to the patchwork cushions and embroidered coverlets on the day-bed.

LEFT The success of this corner is to do with the choice of matt colours, the way in which the pictures are displayed, the dried flowers and the eclectic selection of sundry items, including a rocking horse, fabric cat, 19thC jug and basket with soaps. No one should be afraid to mix the serious with the frivolous.

OPPOSITE This immensely feminine Victorian bedroom makes use of many different linens and textiles. The iron bedstead has been painted the same blue as the Lloyd loom chair. The bed coverings are old quilts, tablecloths and sheets. The curtain has been made from a lacy tablecloth. The round table, covered by a large Victorian crisp white linen tablecloth, has a collection of 19thC porcelain and scent bottles. Note how effective are the old-fashioned roses in the sucrier (sugar bowl).

ABOVE TOP AND BOTTOM Two methods of dealing with a sofa in a period interior. In the first instance (top), a beaten-up old sofa has been draped in a large quilt and covered in cushions. In the second (bottom), the choice has been a good modern sofa built on traditional lines and again covered with cushions.

Creating the look

The Victorian country style is a lighter, simpler version of the Victorian townhouse style. It works particularly well in bedrooms, kitchens and bathrooms. There is less clutter and rooms have a cottagey, timeless quality, very different from the slightly claustrophobic feel of a room in a townhouse of the same period.

COLOURS White and pastel shades – varying in tone from pale through to clear bright – should be offset by occasional touches of darker green, red, blue or black.

WALLS White or pastel colourwashed walls make a good background. You can introduce pattern with stencils. Flowery wallpapers, particularly roses, also work well for this style.

FURNITURE The same rounded shapes are right for upholstery in town or country homes, but for the country look choose less opulent designs and fabrics. Slightly faded loose covers give a pleasant relaxed feel. Mahogany chairs and tables can work just as well in this more casual setting, provided that you choose the less grand designs. Alternatively, opt for plain painted pine cupboards and dressers, again perhaps decorated with stencils. Plainly shaped chairs and tables also look good when painted. If the paint is slightly scuffed, so much the better: a touch of shabbiness suits this style. Windsor chairs set just the right note. Iron or brass bedsteads are a good choice.

SOFT FURNISHINGS Simple muslin or floral-print curtains, sparkling white lace-trimmed tablecloths, crochet or knitted bedspreads and patchwork quilts, set the airy mood of this style.

FLOORING Stripped, polished or stained floorboards with rag rugs on top are appropriate. A good alternative to a rag rug would be a striped cotton dhurrie.

ABOVE This relaxed feminine look has been achieved by covering an armchair with a quilt and cushions (do make sure that the quilt is in good condition) and by draping a table with fabric and lace and the window with a linen tablecloth.

LIGHTING Oil lamps – real or electrified – are a better choice than reproduction gas lamp styles. Choose candles for their decorative appeal and for lighting at mealtimes.

ORNAMENTS Bric-à-brac should be less sophisticated than in a townhouse room, and less abundant. Staffordshire figures, blue-and-white printed pottery, fairings (presents bought at a fair) and samplers would add the right note to this style of room.

FINISHING TOUCHES Throw a patchwork quilt over an old comfortable armchair to blend it into a country room.

Look for authentic period fabrics in antique markets – scraps of old lace and pieces of linen. To take mould stains out of old cotton bedlinen and tablecloths soak them in Nappisan.

Arts and Crafts

LEFT AND OPPOSITE
Gustav Stickley (1857–1942) was one of the most important designers of the later Arts and Crafts style in the Eastern states of America. He not only produced good-quality Arts and Crafts furniture but between 1901 and 1916 edited the *Craftsman* magazine. His furniture is usually made of oak and he was known for his great belief in "simplicity of construction". Most pieces are stamped with the Stickley motto "Als Ik Kan" (All I can). This period of designer craftsmen harked back in some respects to the Shakers, but really had more to do with the English Arts and Crafts movement.

William Morris, who hated mass production and insisted on truth to materials and honesty of design, laid the foundations for the English Arts and Crafts Movement of the 1880s and 1890s. Artists, designers and craftsmen looked back to the Middle Ages as the golden age of craftsmanship and formed themselves into guilds on the medieval pattern. The movement found enthusiastic support in America, where it blossomed as the "Craftsman style".

The emphasis was on craftsmanship, quality of materials and the use of the right material for a specific purpose. Although inspired by the workmanship and sometimes the motifs of the Middle Ages, these designer-craftsmen were not merely aping medieval styles. The furniture and decorative articles they produced were true to a long English tradition; however, the style they created was totally original.

The Arts and Crafts Movement also produced a number of talented architects who worked in an English vernacular style, foreshadowed by Philip Webb who built William Morris' first home. Perhaps the most influential of this group was F.G.A. Voysey, who designed every detail of his houses, down to the pots and pans.

An Arts and Crafts room was light and spacious-looking, often painted all over in white or a pale colour, with natural-coloured wood floors covered with rugs. The furniture was plain and upright and usually made of oak decorated with simple cut-out motifs such as hearts or spearheads. To complement the furniture there were articles in pewter, silver, brass and copper and needlework cushions, curtains and wallhangings executed in yarns coloured with natural vegetable dyes.

Decorative motifs were inspired by nature – birds, animals and flowers. The work of Arts and Crafts artists was later to inspire the Art Nouveau style, whose characteristic sinuous shapes were already beginning to be seen in Arts and Crafts designs, particularly illustration, wallpapers and fabrics.

Walls and Windows

The treatment of walls was closely linked with their structure: features such as the fireplace played a decorative as well as functional role. The whole wall surface (often with a picture rail or high plate shelf) might be painted a uniform pale colour, matching the ceiling. Alternatively, there might be a dado; or part of the wall might be covered with tongued-and-grooved boards, perhaps painted a restful green, to shoulder height. The fireplace surround would be incorporated into the wall treatment: for example, a typical room in Voysey's style would have a fireplace surround taken up to picture-rail height, with a mantelshelf at approximately shoulder level.

ABOVE AND ABOVE RIGHT Andrew and Julie Wadsworth display their collection of Arts and Crafts furniture in a living room painted in four shades of eau de nil and carpeted in a deep blue. It is often argued that Arts and Crafts furniture is best displayed against a white background but this interesting colour choice certainly complements the oak and copper. The pieces, all made by designer-craftsmen, are very special, particularly the Liberty sideboard and the Viennese grandfather clock. The built-in units hold books but also conceal such appliances as hi-fi and TV. The desk and chair are Celtic Arts and Crafts.

OPPOSITE This very typical Arts and Crafts beaten copper fireplace by George Walton was made in 1904. The grate is by the architect Charles Voysey. The picture above the fireplace, *The Cloister and the World*, is by G. Sheridan Knowles, 1901: on its original beaten copper frame the title stands out in relief. The modern pottery ewer by Kate Wickham sits happily on the mantelpiece with an Arts and Crafts bowl and boxes and a pair of candlesticks by Christopher Dresser. One of the other interesting pieces in this room is the brass and steel smoking stand on the right by William Goburg. The lampshade is by Quentin Bell.

Painted walls might be embellished with a hand-painted or stencilled frieze. Arts and Crafts artists such as Voysey and A.H. Macmurdo created wallpapers and fabrics. Window treatments would be of the simplest style: a wooden pole with a length of unlined fabric fluttering in the breeze.

FLOORS

Polished boards topped with rugs were a usual choice.

FURNITURE

Furniture shapes were plain and upright and made by traditional joinery techniques. Native woods were used, particularly oak. Sideboards, chests and the like were usually decorated in simple fashion, with cut-out shapes. Sometimes they were embellished with pewter, brass, ivory or leather.

Settles were a favourite style of seating, as were upright chairs with tall backs, again often decorated with cut-out motifs.

ACCESSORIES

Arts and Crafts Guilds included workers in silver, pewter, leather and brass who produced decorative articles by hand in designs inspired by medieval motifs. One of the notable designers of silverware was C.R. Ashbee, who created some particularly attractive goblets, vases and other pieces set with semi-precious stones.

Typical of the style are mirror frames of beaten copper and candle sconces in brass, imposingly proportioned. Needlework in vegetable-dyed wools made up into table runners and cushions and used to trim window curtains and door curtains would further embellish an Arts and Crafts interior.

Creating the look

Colours The natural vegetable-dye colours associated with the Middle Ages are right for textiles and wallpapers. These reds, greens, blues, old roses and dull gold shades can be set against paintwork in a pale or muted colour – try cream or ivory-white, or the duller, paler shades of green.

Walls Panelling walls with tongued-and-grooved boards to above shoulder level, and finishing the top with a plate shelf, is an excellent way to set the scene. The woodwork can then be painted, or coated with coloured varnish – perhaps a greeny-blue – which allows the grain of the wood to show through. The light oak panelling often seen in houses of the late Victorian period and the first quarter of this century is perfect for this style.

Floors Seal and polish floorboards and top them with small rugs; handmade needlework ones in designs of stylized flowers and animals would be appropriate for this period, or you could choose Morris-style patterns or old oriental rugs. If you have a solid floor, cover it with sisal or rush matting.

Furniture Oak is the material associated with this style. Look for upright chairs with straight backs, and sideboards, chests and settles constructed on straightforward, "honest" lines. Cut-out spearheads and hearts are often the only form of decoration, although larger pieces may have a relief decoration in copper or brass. Plain upright chairs and tables in oak made in the 1930s can be used in conjunction with authentic pieces. Or buy new furniture in the Arts and Crafts style.

Soft furnishings A simple window treatment is best – pairs of curtains hung from wood or brass poles. For upholstery or curtains, choose fabrics by Morris, Voysey and their contemporaries with designs of birds, animals and flowers.

Lighting Concealed general lighting, with candles in pewter or brass candlesticks as the only visible light sources, would suit this style of interior. Alternatively, use Victorian or Edwardian light fittings.

Ornaments Pictures on medieval themes in the Pre-Raphaelite manner work well. Look out too for illustrations by Walter Crane. Rectangular or oval mirror frames in beaten copper, sometimes ornamented with plain semi-precious stones, give an authentic touch. Blend these with pewter or slipware plate, saltglaze jugs and so on.

Finishing touches Fix lengths of curtain pole around the walls of the room at a little above shoulder level and hang suitable fabric from them on rings to softly cover the walls. Appropriate sounds for this look might include Barber's *Adagio for Strings*, Mahler's *Adagio* from *Symphony No. 5*, or *Don Juan* by Richard Strauss.

Opposite The crucial feature of this Arts and Crafts dining room is the choice of colour and the way in which the cream panels frame the mirror and painting. The choice of floral decoration – blue thistles – is very appropriate for this style of interior.

Above left The eau de nil background and the deep matt blue in the foreground help to add warmth to the oak furniture in this room. Spiky, slightly medieval-looking flower arrangements reinforce the period touch. Underfoot is a copy of an 18thC marble floor.

Above right A wonderful piece of stained glass in two tones of blue. Such panels can be bought or commissioned from a stained glass artist, and are certainly more striking and effective than net curtains.

DIRECTORY

INTERIOR DESIGNERS

Bennison Fabrics
16 Holbein Place
London
SW1W 8NL
Tel: 0171 730 8076
Interior designers and fine art dealers, specializing in interesting antique furniture. They carry an imaginative stock of unusual pieces as well as making their own range of "antique" light fittings.

Jane Churchill
151 Sloane Street
London
SW1X 9BX
Tel: 0171 730 9847
Designs combine an 18th- or 19th-century feel with a modern lightness of touch. Paintings and prints used imaginatively.

Colefax and Fowler
19-23 Grosvenor Hill
London
W1X 9HG
Tel: 0181 874 6484
and
110 Fulham Road
London SW3 6RL
Tel: 0171 244 7427
Interior design service as well as practical advice on colour schemes, curtain treatment and upholstery. A wide selection of upholstered furniture, lighting and carpets as well as exclusive chintzes and wallpapers.

Elizabeth Eaton
85 Bourne Street
London
SW1W 8HF
Tel: 0171 730 2262
Offers a full decorator service of advice on interiors of period houses, and the services of a qualified architect renowned for work on period property, joinery and cabinetmaking. Advice on painting and decorating. Also supply period wallpapers and fabrics.

Christophe Gollut
Alistair Colvin Limited
116 Fulham Road
London
SW3 6HU
Tel: 0171 370 4101
Furniture of the 18th and 19th centuries used in eclectic Continental-influenced interiors. Favours a rich, mellow mood.

Jonathan Hudson
16 Fitzjames Avenue
London
W14 ORP
Tel: 0171 602 8829
Specializes in creating elegant interiors in period styles.

Stephen Mack Associates
Chase Hill Farm
Ashaway
Rhode Island
02804
USA
Tel: 401 377 8041
Specializes in the reconstruction and restoration of 17th- and 18th-century buildings.

Anthony Paine
24 Highgate High Street
London
N6 5JG
Tel: 0181 340 4187
Architectural and interior design. Specializes in classical and traditional buildings.

Stuart Interiors
Barrington Court
Ilminster
Somerset
TA19 ONQ
Tel: 01460 240349
See Reproduction Furniture.

Melissa Wyndham
6 Sydney Street
London
SW3
Tel: 0171 352 2874
Every aspect of interior design from rebuilding structures to buying antiques. Colours, curtains, furnishings.

FITTINGS

A Touch of Brass
210 Fulham Road
London
SW10 9PJ
Tel: 0171 351 2255
Solid brass shelf brackets, hooks, door knockers and restoration of period bathroom equipment.

Antique Baths of Ivybridge Ltd
Erme Bridge Works
Ermington Road
Ivybridge
Devon
PL21 9DE
Tel: 01752 698250
Renovation and restoration of authentic antique (Victorian, Edwardian, 1920s & 1930s) baths and suites.

Antique Fireplace Warehouse
194-202 Battersea Park Road
Battersea
London
SW11 4ND
Tel: 0171 627 1410
A selection of period fireplaces.

Architectural Components Ltd
4-8 Exhibition Road
London
SW7 2HF
Tel: 0171 581 2401
Suppliers of English period door furniture, cabinet fittings and bathroom accessories.

Architectural Rescue
1-3 Southampton Way
London
SE5 7JH
Tel: 0171 277 0315
Stockists of original doors, chimneypots, floorboards and some furniture.

Baileys Home and Garden
The Engine Shed
Station Approach
Ross-On-Wye
Herefordshire
HR9 7BW
Tel: 01989 563015
Bathroom fittings, fireplaces, light fittings, door accessories; antique and repro.

Bath Doctor
Prospect House
Canterbury Road
Challock
Ashford
Kent
TN25 4BB
Tel: 01233 740532
Supply and restoration of period bathroom equipment.

Britain's Heritage
Shaftesbury Hall
3 Holy Bones
Leicester
LE1 4LJ
Tel: 0116 251 9592
Specialists in original antique fireplaces, reproductions and accessories.

Chadder & Co
Blenheim Studio
Lewes Road
Forest Row
East Sussex
RH18 5EZ
Tel: 01342 823243
Antique and traditional baths.

Czech & Speake
39c Jermyn Street
London
SW1Y 6DN
Tel: 0171 439 0216
Exclusive bathroom specialist.

Drummonds of Bramley Architectural Antiques Ltd
Birtley Farm
Horsham Road
Bramley
Guildford
Surrey
GU5 OLA
Tel: 01483 898766
Specialists in period bathrooms.

Fron Furniture
Fron Farm
Llanfynydd
Wrexham
LL115 HW
Tel: 01352 770374
Traditional oak doors, floors and beams.

Ideal Standard
The Bathroom Works
National Avenue
Kingston upon Hull
HU5 4HS
Tel: 01482 346461
Makers of bathroom fittings. Wide range of Victorian, Palladian and Art Deco designs.

Illumin Glass Studio
82 Bond Street
Macclesfield
Cheshire
SK11 6QS
Tel: 01625 613600
Makers of stained glass lighting and windows. Renovations of antique light fittings and a selection of original fittings in stock.

The Imperial Bathroom Company
Unit 2
Stag Industrial Estate
Oxford Street
Bilston
West Midlands
WV14 7HZ
Tel: 01902 404111
Period bathroom products.

JD Beardmore & Co Ltd
3-4 Percy Street
London
W1P OEJ
Tel: 0171 637 7041
Architectural hardware in period styles.

Lacy Gallery
203 Westbourne Grove
London
W11 2SB
Tel: 0171 229 6340
Specialists in antique and period picture frames and mirrors.

Lassco
Mark Street
London
EC2A 4ER
Tel: 0171 739 0448
The London Architectural Salvage and Supply Co. Ltd.

Old Fashioned Bathrooms
Little London Hill
Stowmarket
Suffolk
IP14 6PW
Tel: 01728 860926
Specialists in original bathroom fittings – particularly Victorian and Edwardian.

Philip Bradbury Glass
83 Blackstock Road
London
N4 2JW
Tel: 0171 226 2919
Reproductions of patterned acid-etched and stained glass for entrances and areas that require decorative screening.

Randalls Nursery
Lyne Lane
Lyne
Chertsey
Surrey
KT16 OAW
Tel: 0932 566106
Refurbishers of bathroom fittings and accessories.

Sabrina
Alma Street
Mountfields
Shrewsbury
Shropshire
SY3 8QL
Tel: 01743 357977
Handcrafted, traditional oak doors.

The Victorian Ironmonger
The Old Garage
Fosseway
Brinklow
Rugby
Warks
CV23 OLN
Tel: 01788 832292
Stockists of original period house fittings.

Water Front
New Inn Farm
Beckley
Oxon
OX3 9TY
Tel: 01865 351133
Traditional bathroom accessories.

FLOORS & CARPETS

Axminster Carpets Ltd
Axminster
Devon
EX13 5PQ
Tel: 01297 32244
Traditional and period designs.

Bosanquet Ives
3 Court Lodge
48 Sloane Square
London
SW1 8AT
Tel: 0171 730 6241
Design and produce carpets to interior designers' instructions. Also stock jute matting.

Brintons Ltd
PO Box 16
Exchange Street
Kidderminster
Worcestershire
DY10 1AG
Tel: 01562 820000
Traditional designs.

Chatsworth Carpets
227 Brompton Road
London
SW3 2EP
Tel: 0171 584 1386
Period designs, particularly 19th-century.

Fired Earth
Twyford Mill
Oxford Road
Adderbury
Oxon
OX17 3HP
Tel: 01295 812088
and
117-119 Fulham Road
London SW3 6RL
Tel: 0171 589 0489
Handmade terracotta tiles, slate floors, encaustic floor tiles etc.

Mosaics
Elaine M. Goodwin
4 Devonshire Place
Exeter
EX4 6JA
Tel: 01392 270943
Artist specialising in wall and floor mosaics. Materials include gold, Italian glass and smalti.

FURNITURE: ANTIQUE

Cedar Antiques Ltd
63 High Street
Hartley Wintney
Hampshire
RG27 8NT
Tel: 01252 843252
Specialists in country furniture from the 17th and 18th centuries.

H.W. Keil Ltd
Tudor House
Broadway
Worcstershire
WR12 7DP
Tel: 01386 852408
Specialists in 17th- and 18th-century furniture.

John Bly Antiques
27 Bury Street
St James
London
SW1Y 6AL
Tel: 0144 282 3030
Fine antiques bought and sold, full valuations, cabinet making and restoration.

Mallet
Bourdon House Ltd
2 Davies Street
London
W1Y 1LJ
Tel: 0171 629 2444
Fine English furniture and decorative items.

Millers of Chelsea Antiques Ltd
Netherbrook House
86 Christchurch Road
Ringwood
Hampshire
BH24 1DR
Tel: 01425 472062
Fine English period furniture.

Paul Reeves
32B Kensington Church Street
London
W8 4HA
Tel: 0171 937 1594
Furniture and artefacts from 1860 to 1960.

Robert Young Antiques
68 Battersea Bridge Road
London
SW11 3AG
Tel: 0171 228 7847
Specialists in country furniture and folk art.

Rupert Cavendish Antiques
630 Kings Road
London
SW6 2DX
Tel: 0171 731 7041
Specialists in Empire and Biedermeier furniture, and 20th-century paintings.

Seventh Heaven
Chirk Mill
Chirk
Wrexham
Clwyd
LL14 5BU
Tel: 01691 777622
Extensive collection of antique beds – mostly late 19th century.

FURNITURE: REPRODUCTION

Bevan Funnel Limited
Reprodux House
Norton Road
Newhaven
East Sussex
BN9 OBZ
Tel: 01273 513762
Quality reproduction furniture in a variety of period styles.

British Antique Replicas
School Close
Queen Elizabeth Avenue
Burgess Hill
West Sussex
RH15 9RX
Tel: 01444 245577
Period-style furniture.

E.G.Hudson (UK) Ltd
Faraday Close
Worthing
West Sussex
BN13 3PN
Tel: 01903 692211
18th-century-style handmade furniture in mahogany, yewtree, rosewood and walnut.

Lion House Antiques
High Street
Moreton-in-Marsh
Glos.
GL56 0LH
Tel: 01608 652500
Hand-built copies of 18th-century period furniture in oak, pine and mahogany.

The Old Bakery
Punnetts Town
Nr Heathfield
East Sussex
TN21 9DS
Tel: 01435 830608
Designers and makers of traditional furniture and lighting. Also interior design, fabrics and wallpapers.

Over Mantels
66 Battersea Bridge Road
London
SW11 3AG
Tel: 0171 223 8151
Antique and reproduction mirrors and frames.

Oxley's Furniture
Lapstone Barn
Westington Hill
Chipping Campden
Gloucestershire
GL55 6UR
Tel: 01386 840466
Solid aluminium furniture, including dining furniture, chairs, coffee and side tables, in predominantly 19th-century-inspired designs.

The Paul Ferguson Workshop
Workshop 20
21 Wren Street
London WC1X OHF
Tel: 0171 278 8759
Wood carvers and gilders. Specialize in European styling 1670–1820. High-quality reproductions and antiques.

Percy Bass Ltd
184-188 Walton Street
London SW3 2JL
Tel: 0171 589 4853
Reproduction sofas and chairs. Also interior design and antique restoration services.

R & D Davidson
Romsey House
51 Maltravers Street
Arundel
West Sussex
BN18 9BQ
Tel: 01903 883141
Designers & manufacturers of fine furniture in period styles including 18th-century designs, Regency, Art Deco and Biedermeier.

R. Griffiths Woodwear Ltd
Wychwood Design
Viscount Court
Brize Norton
Oxfordshire
OX18 3QQ
Tel: 01993 851435
Furniture design and manufacture. Offers an upholstery service, fine wood decorative products, and giftware.

Rupert Brown
Dean Darm
Woodcutts
Nr Handley
Salisbury
Wiltshire
SP5 5RT
Tel: 017255 552438
Cabinetmaker specializing in period styles.

Stuart Interiors
Barrington Court
Ilminster
Somerset
TA19 ONQ
Tel: 01460 240349
Period furniture, architectural joinery, antiques, textiles, lighting and decorative accessories. Historical research, design, development and consultancy.

Tempus Stet Ltd
Hereford House
Kennington Park
Cranmer Road
London SW9 6EJ
Tel: 0171 820 8666
Reproduction furniture, wall lights, mirrors, curtain finials, pelmets, cartouches, columns and occasional pieces.

William L. Maclean
Hollingbury Industrial Estate
Carden Avenue
Brighton
BN1 8AF
Tel: 01273 565441
Manufacturers of fine-quality furniture, including bergeres, occasional tables, chests, and bookcases.

William Tillman
30 St James's Street
London
SW1A IHB
Tel: 0171 839 2500
Period and reproduction furniture of the 18th and 19th centuries.

LIGHTING

Best & Lloyd
William Street West
Smethwick
West Midlands
B66 2NX
Tel: 121 5581191
Designers and manufacturers of bespoke lighting.

Christopher Wray Lighting Ltd
591/593 Kings Road
London
SW6 2YW
Tel: 0171 736 8434
Repro and period-style lighting.

David Hunt Lighting Ltd
Tileman's Lane
Shipson-on-Stour
Warwickshire
CV36 4HP
Tel: 01608 661 590
Manufacture light fittings for domestic and contractual use. Also restoration and conversion of period lighting.

Jones (Lighting)
194 Westbourne Grove
London
W11 2RH
Tel: 0171 229 6866
The largest selection of individual original lighting (c.1860–1960) in the world. No reproductions.

Sugg Lighting Ltd
65 Gatwick Road
Crawley
Sussex RH10 2YU
Tel: 01293 540111
Manufacturers of gas and electric lighting for exterior use in traditional Victorian and Edwardian styles.

PAINT FINISHES

Cole & Son
142-144 Offard Road
London N1 1NS
Tel: 0171 607 4288
Special paints, including "Georgian Grey" and "Queen Anne White".

Dulux
Wexham Road
Slough
Berkshire SL2 5D
Tel: 01753 550000
Historic Colours range.

Farrow and Ball
Uddens Trading Estate
Dorset BH21 7NL
Tel: 01202 876141
National Trust paint range.

Fired Earth
Twyford Mill
Oxford Mill
Oxford Road
Adderbury
Oxon OX17 3HP
Tel: 01295 812088
and
117-119 Fulham Road
London SW3 6RL
Tel: 0171 589 0489
V&A range of historic colours.

TEXTILES & WALLPAPERS

Alexander Beauchamp
2/12 2nd Floor
Chelsea Harbour
Design Centre
London SW10 OXE
Tel: 0171 376 4556
Design and hand-print wallpapers, including exact character reproductions of historical designs and colourings. Many 19th-century dado papers.

Anna French
343 Kings Road
London
SW3 5ES
Tel: 0171 351 1126
Designs, produces and exports printed and woven fabrics, cotton lace, voiles, wallpapers and borders.

Antique Designs Ltd
Ash House
Ash House Lane
Little Leigh
Northwich
Cheshire
CW8 4RG
Tel: 01606 892822
Bedlinens, bedroom accessories and tablelinens reproduced from Edwardian and Victorian designs.

The Design Archives
PO Box 1464
Bournemouth
Dorset
BH4 9YO
Tel: 01202 753248
Furnishing wholesalers now reproducing some fine old chintzes. Specialities are late 18th- and early 19th-century designs.

Fired Earth
Twyford Mill
Oxford Road
Adderbury
Oxfordshire
OX17 3HP
Tel: 01295 812088
and
117-119 Fulham Road
London
SW3 6RL
Tel: 0171 589 0489
Specialist retailers of interior finishes including fabrics.

The Gainsborough Silk Weaving Co Ltd
Alexandra Road
Sudbury
Suffolk
CO10 6HX
Tel: 01787 372081
High-quality fabrics, wallpaper and trimmings, specializing in silks, cottons and historical designs.

G.P. and J. Baker
P.O. Box 30
West End Road
High Wycombe
Bucks HP11 2QD
Tel: 01494 467467
Wide selection of period fabrics taken from original documents, mainly 18th- and 19th-century. Collections include the National Trust Country House Collection and English Toile Collection.

Hamilton Weston Wallpapers Ltd
10 St Mary's Grove
Richmond
Surrey TW9 1UX
Tel: 0181 940 4850
Specialists in documentary reproductions of wallpapers of the 18th and early 19th century.

John Oliver Ltd
33 Pembridge Road
London
W11 3HG
Tel: 0171 221 6466
Will reproduce wallpapers from client's own sample or design.

Liberty & Co
Regent Street
London
W1
Tel: 0171 734 1234
Art Nouveau, Arts and Crafts and William Morris textiles.

Percheron
Chelsea Harbour
Design Centre
London
SW10 OXE
Tel: 0171 5805156
Importers of furnishing fabrics and trimmings. Traditional damasks, brocades and velours. Also trimmings.

Ramm, Son & Crocker
Chiltern House
The Valley Centre
Gordon Road
High Wycombe
Bucks HP13 6EQ
Tel: 01494 603555
Specialize in the reproduction of original documents, mainly of the 19th century.

Sanderson
100 Acres
Sanderson Road
Uxbridge
Middlesex
UB8 19H
Tel: 01885 238244
Hand-printed papers from original documents, including many by William Morris. Also dado papers.

Tissunique Ltd
Chelsea Harbour
Design Centre
London
SW10 OXE
Tel: 0171 349 0096
Wholesalers and importers of furnishing fabrics and wallpapers, braids and trimmings. Collections cover many periods. Specialists in historic house reproduction work.

Today Interiors
Hollis Road
Grantham
Lincs
NG31 7QH
Tel: 01476 574401
Broderie collection of fabrics, wallpapers and borders, inspired by antique botanical prints, and studies of 18th-century lace panels and trimmings.

Turnell & Gigon Ltd
Chelsea Harbour
Design Centre
London SW10 OXE
Tel: 0171 351 5142
Excellent range of trimmings in a wide range of colours by Passementerie Ile de France. Distributor of Schumacher fabrics.

Warner Fabrics
Bradbourne Drive
Tilbrook
Milton Keynes
Bucks
MK7 8BE
Tel: 01908 366900
Reproductions of period wallpapers and printed fabrics, mainly from the early 1800s. Damasks and woven fabrics dating from the 16th century onwards, in traditional designs.

Watts of Westminster
Chelsea Harbour
Design Centre
London
SW10 OXE
Tel: 0171 376 4486
Hoar Cross Collection of hand-printed Victorian Gothic wall-coverings designed by A.W.N. Pugin and G.F. Bodley. Also woven damasks and tapestries, and stamped velvets.

Zoffany
Talbot House
17 Church Street
Rickmansworth
Herts WD3 1DE
Tel: 01923 710680
and
63 South Audley Street
London
W1Y 5BF
Tel: 0171 495 2505
Manufacturers of document wallpapers, including the hand-printed Temple Newsam Collection. Designs range from mid- and late 18th century to Art Deco.

ANTIQUE TEXTILES

Catherine Shinn Decorative Textiles
7 Suffolk Parade
Cheltenham
Gloucestershire
GL50 2AB
Tel: 01242 574546
Antique textiles including cushions, bell pulls and passementerie.

David Hartwright Ltd
Heraz Shop
2 Halkin Arcade
Motcomb Street
London
SW1X 8JT
Tel: 0171 245 9479
Antique oriental, Aubusson, Needlework and European carpets, tapestries and textile cushions. Specialist cleaning and restoration.

The Gallery of Antique Costumes & Textiles
2 Church Street
London
NW8 8ED
Tel: 0171 723 9981

The Silk Museum
The Heritage Centre
Roe Street
Macclesfield
SK11 6UT
Tel: 01625 613210
Museum devoted to the silk industry, housed in 1813 building.

Toynbee-Clark Interiors Ltd
95 Mount Street
London
W1
Tel: 0171 499 4472/3
Antique 18th- and early 19th-century Chinese export wallpapers, and French panoramic and drapery papers.

Victoria and Albert Museum
Textiles and Dress Department
Exhibition Road
London
SW7 2RL
Tel: 0171 938 8425
Offers an advisory service on the first Tuesday of every month, from 2.30 to 5pm.

COURSES

Inchbald School of Design
Interior Design
7 Eaton Gate
London
SW1W 9BA
Tel: 0171 730 5508
Courses in history and practice of Interior and Garden design.

KLC Interior Design Course
KLC House
Springvale Terrace
London
W14 OAE
Tel: 0171 602 8592
30-week, 4-week and 1- and 3-day courses in Interior Design.

Lyn le Grice
The Flower Loft
Trereife
Penzance
Cornwall
TR20 8TJ
Tel: 01736 364193
One-day stencilling courses in London and one-week courses in Falmouth.

Rhodec International
35 East Street
Brighton
East Sussex
BN1 1HL
Tel: 01273 327476
Home study courses in interior design leading to Diploma in Higher Education.

Sotheby's Educational Studies
30 Oxford Street
London
W1R 1RE
Tel: 0171 462 3232
Courses ranging from one week to one year in the Decorative arts.

V & A Museum
South Kensington
London
SW7 2RL
Tel: 0171 938 8425
The Education Department offers a range of courses and other services for schools and further and higher education.

ASSOCIATIONS

Art Workers Guild
6 Queen Square
London
WC1N 3AR
Tel: 0171 837 3474
Guilds of artists, architects, craftsmen and others engaged in the design and practice of the arts.

Charles Rennie Mackintosh Society
Queen's Cross
870 Garscube Road
Glasgow
G20 7EL
Tel: 0141 946 6600

English Heritage
23 Savile Row
London
W1X 1AB
Tel: 0171 973 3000
Secures the preservation of the country's architectural and archaeological heritage and promotes the public's enjoyment and knowledge of this through the management of more than 350 historic properties in its care.

The Georgian Group
6 Fitzroy Square
London
W1P 6DX
Tel: 0171 387 1720
Gives advice on repair and restoration to owners of Georgian buildings.

The Guild of Master Craftsmen
166 High Street
Lewes
East Sussex
BN7 1XU
Tel: 01273 477374
Trade association helping to put prospective clients in touch with experienced craftsmen able to carry restoration work.

Historic Homes of Britain
21 Pembroke Square
London
W8 6PB
Tel: 0171 937 2402

Historic Houses Association
2 Chester Street
London
SW1X 7BB
Tel: 0171 259 5688

The National Trust
36 Queen Anne's Gate
London
SW1H 9AS
Tel: 0171 222 9251

National Association of Decorative and Fine Arts Societies
Nadsas House
8 Guilford Street
London
WC1N 1DT
Tel: 0171 430 0730

Textile Services Association Ltd
7 Churchill Court
58 Station Road
North Harrow
Middlesex
HA2 7SA
Tel: 0181 863 7755
Can supply addresses of specialists in cleaning and re-glazing old chintz, and cleaning fine linen and antique lace.

The Victorian Society
1 Priory Gardens
Bedford Park
London
W4 1TT
Tel: 0181 994 1019
A conservation amenity group dedicated to the preservation of Victorian and Edwardian buildings.

HISTORIC HOUSES & MUSEUMS

The American Museum in Britain
Claverton Manor
Bath
BA2 7BD
Tel: 01225 460503
Shows, through period rooms, the development of American decorative arts from the late 17th to mid-19th centuries. Also has an extensive collection of quilts and other textiles.

Arbury Hall
Nuneaton
Warwickshire
CV10 7PT
Tel: 01203 382804
Elizabethan house with collections of antique furniture, pictures, glass and china.

Athelhampton House
Athelhampton
Dorchester
Dorset
DT2 7LG
Tel: 01305 848 363
Fine medieval house. Medieval, Tudor and 18th-century rooms.

Barrington Court
Nr Ilminster
Somerset TA19 ONQ
Tel: 01460 241938
Tudor house.

Belton House
Nr Grantham
Lincolnshire
WG32 2LS
Tel: 01476 566116
Restoration house. Grinling Gibbons school carvings.

Boughton Monchelsea Place
Nr Maidstone
Kent
Tel: 01622 743120
Elizabethan house, interior partly remodelled in the Regency period.

Burghley House
Stamford
Lincolnshire
PE9 3JY
Tel: 01780 752451
Fine late Elizabethan house.

Calke Abbey
Ticknall
Nr Melbourne
Derbyshire BE73 1LE
Tel: 01332 865272
House built 1701–1703, contains treasure trove of Victoriana.

Cardiff Castle
Cardiff
South Glamorgan
Wales
Tel: 01222 878100
Gothick dining room.

Castle Coole
Enniskillen
County Fermanagh
BT74 6JY
Northern Ireland
Tel: 01365 322690
Neo-classical house built in 1798 by James Wyatt. Regency furnishings.

Charleston Farmhouse
Lewes
East Sussex
Tel: 01323 811 265
1930s' Bloomsbury group's country home.

Chettle House
Chettle
Blandford
Dorset
Tel: 01258 830209
Queen Anne house with interiors remodelled in the 19th century.

Church Farmhouse Museum
Greyhound Hill
London
NW4 4JR
Tel: 0181 209 1030
Built 1660, with period furnished kitchen (c.1820), dining room (c.1850) and scullery (c.1890).

Claydon House
Middle Claydon
Buckingham
MK18 2EY
Tel: 01296 730349
Georgian house with Rococo, Palladian, Neo-classical and Gothic rooms.

Cragside House
Morpeth
Northumberland
NE65 7PX
Tel: 01669 620333
House designed by Norman Shaw, aesthetic interiors, first house in the world to be lit by electricity generated by water power.

Doddington Hall
Lincoln
LN6 4RU
Tel: 01522 694308
Elizabethan mansion.

Dorney Court
Windsor
Berkshire
Sl4 6QP
Tel: 01628 604638
Elizabethan manor house.

18 Folgate Street
Spitalfields
London
Tel: 0171 2474013
House built in 1724 with rooms furnished and decorated in styles from 1724 to the early 20th century.

Forde Abbey
Chard
Somerset
TA20 4LU
Tel: 01460 220 231
Cromwellian country house.

Geffrye Museum
Kingsland Road
London E2 8EA
Tel: 0171 739 9893
Period rooms from 1600 to the present day.

Gainsborough Old Hall
Parnell Street
Gainsborough
Lincoln
DN21 2NB
Tel: 01427 612669
One of the best preserved medieval manor houses in the country.

Hagley Hall
Hagley
Nr Stourbridge
DY9 9LG
Tel: 01562 882408
Home of the 11th Viscount Cobham. Palladian house with rich Rococo decoration.

Hardwick Hall
Doe Lea
Chesterfield
Derby S44 IQJ
Tel: 01246 850430
Elizabethan house.

Holkham Hall
Wells-Next-to-Sea
Norfolk
NR23 1AB
Tel: 01328 710227
Fine Palladian mansion.

Keddleston Hall
Derby DE22 SJH
Tel: 01332 842191
House designed by Robert Adam.

Kelmscott Manor
Nr Lechlade
Gloucestershire
Tel: 01367 252486
16th-century Cotswold manor. Summer house of William Morris. Original Morris possessions and designs.

Knole Park
Sevenoaks
Kent
Tel: 01732 450608
Splendid Jacobean interior.

Lacock Abbey
Nr Chippenham
Wiltshire FN1S 2LG
Tel: 01249 730227
Georgian Gothick interiors.

Layer Marney Tower
Near Colchester
Essex CO5 9US
Tel: 01206 330784
Tudor house built in 1520. Open to the public Sundays and weekdays, April to September.

Linley Sambourne House
Leighton House Museum
18 Stafford Terrace
London W8
Tel: 0171 937 0663 (enquiries)
Late Victorian townhouse with preserved aesthetic interior.

The Mackintosh House
Hunterian Art Gallery
University of Glasgow
82 Hillhead Street
Glasgow G12 8QQ
Tel: 0141 330 5431
Reconstruction of main interiors of Charles Rennie Mackintosh's home.

Marble Hill House
Richmond Road
Twickenham
Middlesex
TW1 2NL
Tel: 0181 892 5115
Palladian villa.

Medieval Merchant's House
58 French Street
Southampton
Tel: 01703 221503
House built in 1290, recently restored and refurbished in appropriate style.

Number 1, Royal Crescent
Bath BA1 2LR
Tel: 01225 428126
Restored Georgian house, furnished as an 18th-century home.

Osterley Park House
Osterley
Middlesex
Tel: 0181 560 3918
Fine Adam interiors.

Pallant House
9 North Pallant
Chichester
West Sussex
PO19 1TJ
Tel: 01243 774557
Queen Anne merchant's house.

Parham House
Pulborough
West Sussex RH20 4HS
Tel: 01903 742021
Elizabethan house.

Petworth House
Petworth
West Sussex
GU28 OAE
Tel: 01798 342476
William and Mary house, Grinling Gibbons school carvings.

Preston Manor
Preston Drove
Brighton
BN1 6SD
Tel: 01273 292770
Georgian house, furnished in Edwardian style.

Queen's House
Greenwich
London
SE10 9NF
Tel: 0181 858 4422
Designed by Inigo Jones.

Saltram House
Plympton
Plymouth PL7 3UH
Tel: 01752 336546
Georgian mansion, complete with its original contents. Includes Adam-designed rooms, portraits by Kauffmann and Reynolds and work by Chippendale and Wedgwood.

Sir John Soane's Museum
13 Lincoln's Inn Fields
London WC2A 3BP
Tel: 0171 405 2107
Regency house built by Sir John Soane.

St Mary's
Bramber
West Sussex
BN44 3WE
Tel: 01903 816205
Historic house, includes Elizabethan Painted Room with trompe l'oeil murals.

Stourhead House
Stourton
Warminster
Wiltshire
BA12 6QH
Tel: 01747 840348
Palladian mansion built in the 1720s, designed by Colen Campbell.

Squerryes Court
Westerham
Kent TN16 1SJ
Tel: 01959 562345
17th-century manor house, home to the Warde family since 1731. Collection of Italian 17th-century Dutch, and 18th-century English paintings, furniture, tapestries and porcelain.

Syon House
Brentford
Middlesex
Tel: 0181 560 0881
Fine Adam interiors.

Thornbury Castle
Thornbury
Nr Bristol
S. Gloucestershire
BS35 1HH
Tel: 01454 281182
Castle built by the 3rd Duke of Buckingham and seized by Henry V111. Mullioned windows, stone fireplaces, panelled dining room, paintings, antiques and tapestries.

Waddesdon Manor
Nr Aylesbury
Bucks HP18 0JH
Tel: 01296 651282
French Renaissance-style château housing the Rothschild Collections. Includes French Royal furniture, Savonnerie carpets and portraits by Gainsborough and Reynolds.

Walpole's House, Strawberry Hill
St. Mary's University College
Strawberry Hill
Twickenham
Middlesex TW1 4SX
Tel: 0181 2404114
Gothic Revival building. By appointment only.

Wilton House
The Estate
Wilton
Salisbury
Wiltshire
Tel: 0172 274 4447
Inigo Jones Palladian architecture. Also, Gothick cloisters by James Wyatt, Kent and Chippendale furniture and large art collection.

PLACES WITH STYLE

Burgh Island
Bigby-on-sea
South Devon
TQ7 4BG
Tel: 01548 810514
Hotel restored to its original 1929 Art Deco design. Accessible on foot at low tide.

Clifton House
Nairn
IV12 4HW
Scotland
Tel: 01667 453119
Victorian house containing antiques, objects d'art, paintings and books.

Dorset Square Hotel
39-40 Dorset Square
London
NW1 6QN
Tel: 0171 7237874
The main architectural features of the 1815 residences have been retained. The interior features and decor are a clever mix of old and repro which works well.

Ettington Park Hotel
Alderminster
Stratford-upon-Avon
CV37 8BU
Tel: 01789 450123
A splendid Victorian Gothic mansion, parts of which date back to the Middle Ages. Exquisite drawing room with gilded ceilings and grand piano. Fine antiques and original paintings.

Inverlochy Castle
Torlundy
Fort William
PH33 6SN
Scotland
Tel: 01397 702177
A magnificent castle much admired by Queen Victoria. Crystal chandeliers, frescoed ceiling in the great hall, antiques and paintings.

The Bath Priory
Weston Road
Bath
BA1 2XT
Tel: 01225 331922
Elegant Georgian hotel with period furnishings.

Ston Easton Park
Ston Easton
Chewton Mendip
Nr Bath
Somerset
BA3 4DF
Tel: 01761 241631
A fine Palladian mansion with magnificent 18th-century interiors. Trompe l'oeil murals, antiques, paintings and period bedrooms with four- poster beds.

Dennis Severs
18 Folgate Street
Spitalfields
London E1 6BX
Tel: 0171 247 4013
A unique form of theatre. Guests are escorted into candle-lit chambers from which, apparently, their 18th- and 19th-century inhabitants have just withdrawn. Book at least 3 weeks in advance.

BIBLIOGRAPHY

The Antiques Directory: Furniture, Judith and Martin Miller (Gen. Ed.), Mitchell Beazley, 1985

Authentic Decor – The Domestic Interior 1620-1920, Peter Thornton, Weidenfeld, 1985

The Curtain Book, Caroline Clifton-Mogg and Melanie Paine, Mitchell Beazley, 1988

Displaying Pictures, Caroline Clifton-Mogg and Piers Feetham, Mitchell Beazley, 1988

English Country Houses – Caroline 1625-1685, Oliver Hill and John Cornforth, Antique Collectors Club, 1985

English Country Houses – Baroque 1685-1715, James Lees-Milne, Antique Collectors Club, 1986

English Country Houses – Early Georgian 1715-1760; Mid Georgian 1760-1800; Late Georgian 1800-1840, Christopher Hussey, Antique Collectors Club, boxed set 1988

The English Mediaeval House, Margaret Wood, Ferndale Editions, 1981

E.W. Godwin, Furniture and Interior Decoration, Elizabeth Aslin, John Murray, 1986

The History of Interior Decoration, Charles McCorquodale, Phaidon Press, 1983

Charles Rennie Mackintosh, The Complete Furniture, Furniture Drawings and Interior Design, Roger Billcliffe, John Murray, 1986

The Penguin Dictionary of Decorative Arts, John Fleming and Hugh Honour, 1979

Miller's Pocket Antiques Fact File, Judith and Martin Miller, Mitchell Beazley, 1988

The Penguin Dictionary of Architecture, John Fleming, Hugh Honour and Nikolaus Pevsner, 1966

Period Details, Judith and Martin Miller, Mitchell Beazley, 1986

The Potterton Book of Curtain and Drapery Designs, Potterton Books, Sessay, North Yorks.

Victorian Furniture, R.W. Symonds and B.B. Whineray, Studio Editions, 1987

GLOSSARY

Acanthus Leaf motif, originally used on Greek architecture.

Balloon-back A type of chair with a hooped back, typical of the later 19thC.

Baroque A theatrical, exuberant style, originating in 17thC Italy.

Bird's eye maple Wood of the sugar maple with a distinctive pattern created by aborted buds.

Blue and white A style of underglaze ceramics decoration, originating in China.

Bombé A term applied to the outswelling curves of furniture in the Rococo style.

Bonheur du jour A small writing table on tall legs.

Boulle Marquetry in tortoiseshell and brass.

Brocade A rich fabric with an embossed design, originally in gold or silver. The term has come to mean any flowered fabric with a raised pattern.

Brocatelle A brocade-like fabric, usually of silk or wool.

Cabriole leg A leg, particularly a chair leg, that curves in a shallow S.

Carver A dining chair with arms.

Ceiling rose A circular moulding in the centre of a ceiling, from which a chandelier might be hung.

Chiffonier A low or side cupboard, the upper part having one or two shelves.

Chinoiserie The use of pseudo-Chinese motifs in fabrics, furniture, etc.

Chintz A cotton fabric, usually glazed, printed in colourful patterns of flowers, fruit and birds. The term was originally applied to painted calico from India.

Classical Orders A repertoire of treatments for columns and the entablatures that surmount them. Derived from Ancient Greek temples, the Orders have had a major influence on architecture, furniture and interiors in Europe and North America.

Commode A chest of drawers in the French style.

Console table A table on a large bracket, set against a wall.

Corinthian One of the Classical Orders. The capitals are bell-shaped, with acanthus leaves.

Cornice A decorative moulding at the top of a wall, just below the ceiling.

Court cupboard A cupboard with the lower stage open.

Crewelwork Designs in worsted on a cloth or linen ground.

Dado The lower few feet of a wall, when treated differently from the area of wall above.

Damask A silk or linen fabric with a woven textural pattern.

Delft Tin-glazed earthenware from Holland, usually blue and white. When used without a capital initial, the word applies to English earthenware in the same style.

Dentil A small moulding in the shape of a block.

Doric The plainest of the Classical Orders.

Ebonized A term applied to light-coloured wood stained to the colour of ebony.

Egg-and-dart A form of architectural moulding.

Entablature Decorative band above a row of columns, made up of architrave, frieze and cornice.

***Faux* finish** A surface finish intended to imitate a material such as wood or marble.

Frieze A band across the upper part of a wall, just below the cornice. Also, the middle part of an entablature.

Galloon Narrow close-woven braid.

Girandole A circular wall mirror in a carved gilt frame.

Gothick Pseudo-Medieval style of the 18th and 19thC.

Greek key pattern A band of geometric ornament, in a maze-like design.

Half-tester A rectangular canopy above a bed, extending part-way down the bed from the headboard.

Infill The area of a wall between the dado and frieze.

Inlay The setting of one material (especially a wood) in or over another. Marquetry is one type of inlay.

Ionic One of the Classical Orders. The columns are fluted and the capitals have scrolls, or volutes.

Japanning A Western imitation of oriental lacquering.

Kelim A Middle-Eastern tapestry-woven rug.

Lambrequin A stiff, shaped surround to a window, like an extended pelmet.

Majolica Victorian earthenware with a thick, coloured glaze.

Marquetry See inlay.

Mullions Uprights dividing a window into sections.

Ormolu Any mount, sconce or other article that is gilt or at least gold-coloured.

Ottoman A cushioned seat like a sofa without arms.

Palladian An architectural style derived from that of Andrea Palladio, the 16thC Italian architect.

Parquet Flooring made up of pieces of wood in a geometrical pattern.

Pediment A gabled top over a portico, door or piece of furniture.

Pembroke table A small table with short drop leaves.

Pilaster A shallow pier or column set against a wall.

Press cupboard A cupboard with upper and lower sections both closed by doors.

Rococo A lively, delicate 18thC style, often asymmetrical, with S-shaped curves.

Satinwood An exotic close-grained hardwood, yellow to golden in colour.

Sconce Wall light with candle-holders.

Stencilling A method of decoration, usually to make a repeated pattern, in which paint is brushed over a cut-out design.

Strapwork Decoration of interlaced bands and forms similar to cut leather.

Ticking Stout striped material of linen or cotton.

Toile de Jouy A fabric with pictorial scenes printed in one colour on a cream background.

Treen Small objects made of wood.

Turkeywork Upholstery, cushions, etc, knotted in the manner of Near Eastern rugs.

Wainscot Wood panelling on an internal wall.

Whatnot A stand with three or more shelves.

Windsor chair A country-style chair with a spindled back.

INDEX

Page numbers in *italic* refer to the illustrations.

A

Adam, Robert 53, 57
Adam style *60*
Aesthetic interiors 153
Aga cookers *77*, 159
Albrizzi table 59
Alma-Tadema, Sir Lawrence *150*
American Museum, Bath 72, *78*, 160
American styles
  17thC Country House 24
  Colonial 80-91
  Empire 131-142, 131
  Federal 70-73
  Gothic *167*, 168
  Greek Revival *70*, 131, 132
  Queen Anne 38
  William and Mary 35
Anderson, Lee *167*, *168*, *169*
Art Deco 52
Art Nouveau 178
Arts and Crafts Movement 178-183
Ashbee, C.R. 180
Aubusson carpets *110*, *112*, 120
Axminster carpets 46, 54

B

Back-stools 15
Balloon-back chairs 148
Banister-back chairs *84*, *87*
Barley-twist legs 37
Baroque styles 32-37, 98-117
Basaltware *57*
Bathrooms *65*, *164*, *165*, *175*
Bauhaus furniture 43
Beds/bedrooms
  17thC Country House 23, *28*
  American Colonial 80, *87*, *88*, 91
  American Empire *136*, *137*
  American Federal 72, 73, 136
  Baroque/Rococo 105
  Elizabethan/Jacobean 12, *15*, *28*
  Empire 65, *160*
  Georgian *51*, *64*, *65*
  Queen Anne *38*, *39*
  Regency *122*
  Shaker *94*, *97*
  Victorian *65*, 148, *160*, *162*, *176*
Beech 129
Bell, Quentin *180*
Benches 12, 24
Biedermeier styles *138*
Blackamoor figures *106*, *109*
Blinds 91, *115*, 143, 148
Blue and white wares 37, *110*, 117, *148*, 152, 177
Blue John stone 57
Bonheurs du jour 57
Bookcases 59, *70*, *132*
Boucher, François 100
Boudine *167*
Boulle, Andre-Charles 100, *112*
Boulton, Matthew *57*
Brackets, wall *36*, *110*, *111*, 117
Bramber, Sussex 12
Brass 23, 38, 122, 151, 180
Brewster armchairs 24
Bronze 31, 109, 129, 152, *160*
Brussels carpets 120, 132
Buffets 8, 23
Bureaux 36, 43
Burr maple 129

C

Cabinets *125*
Cabriole legs 38, 43, 49, 103
Candelabra *49*, 72, 100, *109*, *121*
Candles/candlesticks
  17thC Country House *19*, *21*, 23, 31, *31*
  American Colonial *87*
  American Federal 72
  Arts and Crafts *180*, 183
  Baroque/Rococo *116*
  Empire 129
  English Baroque 32, *35*, 37
  Queen Anne *41*, 43, *43*
  Regency 122
  Shaker *94*
  Victorian 177
Carl Johan style *119*
Carpets 8
  18thC Country 74
  American Empire *131*, 143
  American Federal 70
  Baroque/Rococo *103*, *110*, 119
  English Baroque 35
  Georgian 44, 54
  Regency 120, *125*, *132*
  Victorian 151, 171
Carver chairs 24
Ceilings
  17thC Country House 21
  18thC Country 74
  American Colonial *86*, 91
  American Federal 70
  Arts and Crafts 178
  Elizabethan/Jacobean 12
  English Baroque 32
  Georgian 46, *53*
  Regency 118, 120, *125*
Chair rails *95*, 97
Chairs
  17thC American Country House 24, *24*
  17thC Country House *18*, 21, 23, 23
  18thC Country 74, *78*
  American Colonial 80, *84*, *86*
  American Empire 131, *136*
  American Federal *70*, *71*, 72, *73*
  Arts and Crafts *183*
Chairs (continued)
  Baroque/Rococo *100*, *102*, 103, *105*, *106*, *110*, *112*, *114*
  Elizabethan/Jacobean *10*, 12, *14*, *15*
  Empire 129, *129*
  English Baroque *32*, *34*, *36*, *37*
  Georgian *47*, 49, *49*, *50*, *51*, *54*, *57*, *64*, *66*
  Modern *36*, *54*
  Queen Anne *41*, 43
  Regency *108*, 118, *118*, *120*, *125*, *127*, *132*, *135*, *140*
  Shaker 92, *93*, *95*, *97*
  Victorian 147, *150*, 152, *153*, *157*, *162*, *163*, *167*, *169*, 171, *173*, 177, *177*
Chaise longues *120*, 129, 152, *154*
Chandeliers *11*, *50*
  American Federal *70*, 72
  Baroque/Rococo *106*, *108*
  Empire *129*
  English Baroque 35, *37*
  Victorian *155*
Chelsea porcelain *57*
Chests
  17thC American Country House 24
  17thC Country House *21*
  American Colonial *87*, 91
  American Empire *140*
  Arts and Crafts 180
  Elizabethan/Jacobean 15
  Georgian *64*
  Shaker *93*
  Victorian *151*
Chests-of-drawers 23, 43, *64*, 91
Chests-on-stands *36*, *39*
Chiffoniers 122, 151
Chilston Park Hotel, Kent *105*, *173*
"Chinese Chippendale" *52*
Chinese porcelain *23*, *31*, *37*, *46*
Chinoiserie 18, *34*, 44, 46, 61, 100, 118
Chippendale, Thomas 47, *51*, *52*, 57, *59*, 61, 153
Churchill, Jane *148*, 162
Clocks 15, 100, *112*, *126*, 180
Coalport 152
Coffee tables *62*
Coffers *13*, 114
Colbert, Jean Baptiste 100
Colefax and Fowler wallpaper *112*
Collections 171, *172*, *173*
Colour
  17thC Country House *19*, *26*, 31
  American Colonial *80-83*, 91
  American Empire *136*, *142*, 143
  Arts and Crafts *182*, 183
  Baroque/Rococo *104*, *110*, 117
Colour (continued)
  English Baroque *34*
  Georgian 44, *49*, *52*, *53*, *54*, *56*, *57*, *59*, *61*, *63*, *67*
  Queen Anne *42*, 43, *43*
  Regency 118, *125*, *126*
  Shaker *93*, 97
  Victorian *146*, *147*, 148, 171, 177
Commodes *73*, 100, *102*, 103, *109*, *128*, *147*
Concealment of modern equipment *87*
Console tables 44, 47
Copeland porcelain 152
Copenhagen porcelain 66
Copper 180, *181*, 183
Country House styles (17thC) 18-31
Country styles *26*, *162*, *175*
  18thC 74-97
  Early 19thC American *136*
  Victorian 177
"Craftsman" style (America) 178
Crane, Walter 183
Crapaud chairs 103
Creamware *54*, 57
Crewelwork *14*, *28*, *39*, *161*
"Cromwellian" chairs 24
Cupboards
  17thC Country House 23, 24
  American Colonial 80
  American Federal *70*
  Biedermeier *136*
  Elizabethan/Jacobean 15
  Queen Anne 43
  Shaker 92, *95*
  Victorian *167*
  William and Mary 35
Curtains
  17thC Country House 21
  18thC Country *76*
  19thC Classicism 104, *104*
  American Colonial 80, 91
  American Empire *136*, 143
  American Federal *71*
  Arts and Crafts 178, 183
  Baroque/Rococo 104, *104*
  Empire 129
  English Baroque 35, *37*
  Georgian 46, 52, 54, 61
  Queen Anne 43
  Regency *125*
  Shaker 97
  Victorian 147, *162*, 171, 177
Cushions 15, 24, *24*, *102*, *148*, *149*, *154*

D

Dados 43, 61, 147, 178
Davenport desks 151
David, Jacques Louis 103
Davis, A.J. *167*
Day-beds 129
Deer Park Parlor (American Museum, Bath) *71*
Dehn, Hannerle *117*
Delftware *25*, *31*, 32, *34*, *37*, *38*, 46
Derby porcelain *57*, 122
Desks 80, *86*
Distressed finishes 91
Dornix fabrics 19
Dorset Square Hotel, London *154*, *161*
"Dragged" effects 43, 91, *164*
Dresser, Christopher *181*
Dressers *21*, *26*, *31*, 74, *77*, *78*
Dressing tables 23, *162*, *163*
Duchesse brise *115*
Ducks, decoy *80*, *90*, 91

E

Electroplating 152
Elizabethan styles 8-17, 147, 148
Elkington plate 152
Empire styles 129-143
Encoignures 100, 103
Etruscan style 53

F

Fabrics
  17thC American Country House 24
  17thC Country House 19
  18thC Country 74, *76*
  American Colonial 80, *91*
  American Empire 143
  Arts and Crafts 183
  Baroque/Rococo *100*, 117
  Elizabethan/Jacobean 12, *14*, 17
  Empire 129, *135*
  English Baroque 37
  Georgian 43, 46, *49*, *59*, 61, *66*
  Queen Anne *38*, *39*, *41*, 43
  Regency 118, 120
  Victorian *144*, *145*, 147, *147*, *148*, *152*, *154*, *160*, *162*, *163*, *165*, *167*, 170, *171*, *175*, 177, *177*
"Farthingale" chairs 15
Faux finishes 37, *95*, 120, *125*, *127*, *129*
Fireplaces
  18thC Country *76*
  American Colonial 80, *80*, *87*
  American Empire 132, *136*
  Arts and Crafts 178, *181*
  Baroque/Rococo *98*, *109*
  Georgian *46*, *58*
  Regency *124*, *126*
  Victorian *172*
Firescreens *144*
Floorcloths 43, 46, 54, *57*, 70, 74, 151
Floors
  17thC American Country House 24
  17thC Country House 21, *23*
  18thC Country 74, *78*
  American Colonial 80, *84*, *86*, *87*, 91, 91
Floors (continued)
  American Empire 143
  American Federal 70, *70*, *71*
  Arts and Crafts 180, 183, 183
  Baroque/Rococo 104, *108*
  Elizabethan/Jacobean 12, 17
  English Baroque 35, 37
  Georgian 43, 44, 46, 54, *59*, *68*
  Queen Anne 43
  Regency 120, *124*, *127*, 132
  Shaker 97
  Victorian 148, 151, *152*, *158*, *160*, *170*, 171, 177
Fortuny *100*, 117
Friezes 26, 61, *118*, 147, *152*, *154*, *175*, *180*
Furniture
  17thC American Country House 24, *24*, *25*
  17thC Country House *20*, 21, *21*, *22*, *23*, *23*, *26*, *27*, *29*, *30*
  18thC Country 74, *74*, *75*, *76*
  19thC Classical 103-104, 119
  American Colonial *80-87*, 90, 91, *91*
  American Empire 131, 143
  American Federal *70*, *71*, 72
  Arts and Crafts 178, 180, 183
  Baroque/Rococo *98*, 100, *102*, *110*, *114*, 117, 119
  Elizabethan/Jacobean 12, *13*, 15, 16
  Empire 129
  English Baroque *34*, *35*, *36*, *37*, *37*
  Georgian *44*, *45*, 47, *47-69*
  Queen Anne 38, *39*, *41*, *42*, 43, *43*
  Regency 118, 120, 122, *125*
  Shaker *96*, 97
  Victorian 37, 147, 148, *150*, 151, *152*, *160*, *170*, 171, 177
  William and Mary *35*

G

Gas lamps 171
Georgian style 43-69
Gilding 103
Gilt wood furniture *106*, *112*, *115*, 117
Glassware
  Baroque/Rococo *100*, *110*
  Elizabethan/Jacobean 15
  English Baroque 35
  Georgian 66
  Victorian *151*, *167*
Gobelins tapestries 100
Gollut, Christophe *146*, *147*
Gothick styles 46, 118, 147, 148, *157*, *164*, *167*, *168*, *173*
Gumb, Linda *155*

H

Hall-stands 151
Hallways
  American Colonial *82*

- Hallways (continued)
  - American Empire *132, 138,* 140
  - American Federal *70*
  - Baroque/Rococo *100, 109*
  - Georgian *68, 69*
  - Regency *118, 125, 132*
  - Victorian *144, 163*
  - Hart Room (New York Metropolitan Museum of Art) 24
- Haynes Grange Room (Victoria and Albert Museum) 19
- Hepplewhite furniture 57, 72, 118
- Hockin, Kenneth *140, 141*
- Hogarth, William 43
- Hudson, Jonathan *144, 145*

I

- Imari ware *110*

J

- Jacob, George *102*
- Jacobean styles 8-16
- Jasperware *57*
- Jennens and Bettridge 151
- Jenrette, Richard *131, 132, 134, 135, 137, 142*
- Jones, Inigo 18, 19, 44
- Jumel, Madame *143*

K

- Kangxi porcelain *37*, 110
- Kitchens
  - 18thC Country *75, 77, 78, 79*
  - American Colonial *84, 87*, 91
  - Victorian *158, 159*
  - Knifeboxes 66
  - Knowles, G. Sheridan *181*

L

- Lacquerwork 19, 31, 35, 37, 100, *114*, 122
- Ladderback chairs 74, *76, 77, 79, 86*, 91, *93, 94*
- Le Brun, Charles 100
- Lely, Sir Peter *157*
- Lieber, Ian *154*
- Lighting
  - 17thC Country House 23
  - American Colonial 80, 91
  - American Empire 143
  - Arts and Crafts 183
  - Baroque/Rococo 100
  - Elizabethan/Jacobean *11*, 17
  - Empire 129
  - English Baroque 35, 37
  - Queen Anne 43
  - Regency 118, *121*, 122
  - Victorian 148, 151, 171, 177
- Linley Sambourne House *144*
- Lloyd Loom chairs 177
- Lolling chairs 72
- Loo tables 122
- Louis XIV styles 98, 100, 112
- Louis XV styles 100, 103, 114, 115, 147, *147*, 148, *160*
- Lowboys *23*
- Lyre-back chairs *73, 163*

M

- Mack, Stephen *85*
- Macmurdo, A.H. 180
- Mahogany 47, 131, 151, 171
- Mallard, Prudent *160*
- Maple 122
- Martha Washington chairs 72
- Mary II, Queen 32
- Mauchline ware *173*
- Medieval styles 148, *162*, 178
- Meeks, Joseph *140, 167*
- Meissen figures 57, 100
- Metropolitan Museum of Art, American Wing 131-132
- Minton porcelain 152
- Mirrors
  - American Empire *133*, 143
  - American Federal *71*
  - Arts and Crafts 183
  - Baroque/Rococo 100, *105, 106, 108*, 117
  - Georgian 61
  - Queen Anne 43
  - Regency 122, *122, 126, 133, 140*
  - Victorian 148, *154, 160*
- Moorfields carpets 54
- Morris, William 148, 171, 178
- Mortlake tapestries *98*

N

- Nailsea glass 151
- Napoleonic bee design *128*, 129, 135
- Needlework 8, *15, 41*, 178, 180
- Neo-classicism 53, 70

O

- Oak 151, 178, 180, 183
- Oil lamps 122, 129, 143, 151, 177
- Ormolu 122, *126*, 132
- Ornaments
  - Arts and Crafts 183
  - Elizabethan/Jacobean 17
  - English Baroque 37
  - Georgian 61
  - Queen Anne 43
  - Victorian 171, 177
- Osborne and Little wallpapers 74, *152*
- Osterley Park, Middlesex 53
- Ottomans 152, 171

P

- Paintwork
  - 17thC Country House 19, *24*
  - 18thC Country *74*
  - American Colonial *74, 86, 87, 91*
  - American Empire *136*
  - American Federal *71*, 72, *73*
  - Arts and Crafts *180*
- Paintwork (continued)
  - Baroque/Rococo *104, 106, 110*
  - Elizabethan/Jacobean *8*, 12
  - English Baroque *32, 34, 37*
  - Georgian *49, 50, 51, 57, 61*
  - Queen Anne *41*
  - Regency 118, 120, *125, 135*
  - Shaker 92, *95*
  - Victorian *147*, 148, *158, 160, 163*
- Palladian style 38, 44
- Panelling
  - 17thC Country House *18*, 19
  - 18thC American 24
  - 18thC Country 74
  - American Colonial 80, 80, *87*
  - American Empire *136*
  - American Federal *71*
  - Arts and Crafts 183
  - Elizabethan/Jacobean 8, *9, 11*, 12
  - English Baroque 32, *32, 34*, 37
  - Georgian 43, *47, 49, 54, 57, 61*
  - Queen Anne *40, 41*, 43
  - Regency *122*
  - Victorian *165*
- Papier mâché 151
- Parham House, W. Sussex *9, 14, 16, 126*
- Parquet 12, 35, 104, 171
- Patchwork 24, *28, 73, 136, 162, 163, 177*
- Pedestal tables 122, *125*, 151
- Pelmets 35, 37, 43, 52, 54, 61, 70, 148, *162*, 171
- Pembroke tables *57, 64, 71*
- Persian carpets *124, 132*
- "Petticoat" tables *133*
- Pewter *13*, 15, *18*, 24, *97*, 178
- Phyfe, Duncan *134, 135*
- Plas Teg, North Wales *112, 120-123*
- Plasterwork 21, 32, *32*, 44, 53, 74, *81, 91, 152*
- Pompadour, Madame de 100
- Porcelain *57*
  - 17thC Country House *23, 31*
  - 18thC Country *77*
  - American Federal 70, *70*, 72
  - Baroque/Rococo 102, 103, *106, 110*, 117, 119
  - Empire 129
  - English Baroque 37, *37*
  - Georgian 53, 54, *57, 65, 66*
  - Queen Anne *38, 39*, 43, *43*
  - Regency *125*
  - Victorian *148*, 152, *152, 160, 177*
- Pottery
  - 17thC 24, *31*
  - American Colonial *84*
  - Elizabethan/Jacobean 15
  - English Baroque 35
  - Queen Anne 43, *53*
  - Victorian *78, 158, 160, 163*, 171, *173*
- Presses (cupboards) 15
- Prie-dieux 152
- Pugin, A.W. N. 148

Q

- Qianlong porcelain 23, *37*
- Queen Anne styles 38-43, 153
- Quilts 73, *87*, 91, 136

R

- Regency styles 118-128
- Riddell, Crawford *167*
- Robinson, Gerrard 151
- Rococo styles 44, 46, 61, 91, 98-117, 147, 160
- Rosewood 120, 131
- Roux designs *167*, 169
- Rugs 183
  - 17thC Country House 21, *30*, 31
  - American Colonial *87, 90*
  - American Federal *73*
  - Arts and Crafts 183
  - Queen Anne 43, 46, *49*
  - Regency *132*
  - Shaker 97
  - Victorian *151, 165*, 171
- Rush lights *11, 28*
- Rush matting *11*, 21, *76*, 91, 183

S

- Sabre legs 129
- Samplers *28*
- Satinwood 54, 151, 153
- Savonnerie carpets 35, 37, 46
- Scotch carpets 46
- Screens *21*, 35
- Settles 180
- Severs, Dennis *33, 34, 44, 45*
- Sevres porcelain *57*, 117, 129
- Shaker style 92-97
- Sheffield Plate 152
- Sheraton *57, 70, 71*, 72, 122, *135, 136*
- Shutters 49, *49, 50, 57*
- Sideboards 57, *66*, 74, 122, 148, 151, *167, 170, 180*
- Silver furniture 100
- Silverware 23, 35, 37, 38, *41*, 72, 103, 151, 152, 180
- Sofa tables 122
- Sofas
  - American Empire 131, 138
  - Empire *128, 147*
  - Victorian 152, 171, *177*
- Southport, Connecticut *71*
- Spode ware 122
- Spoon-back chairs 152
- Staffordshire figures 152, *170*, 171, 177
- Stained glass 183
- Stencilling *72, 77*, 80, 143, *175, 177*
- Stickley, Gustav *178, 179*
- Swedish Empire style *128*

T

- Table lamps 43, *61*
- Tables
  - 17thC American Country House 24
  - 17thC Country House *19, 20, 21, 23, 37*
  - 18thC Country *78*
  - American Colonial 91
  - American Empire 131, *136*, 140
  - American Federal 70, *71*
  - Arts and Crafts 183
  - Baroque/Rococo *106, 108, 112, 114*
  - Edwardian *49*
  - Elizabethan/Jacobean *10*, 15
  - English Baroque *37*
  - Georgian 47, 49, *57, 59, 61, 64, 66*
  - Queen Anne *41*, 43
  - Regency 118, *118, 121*, 122, *122, 125, 127, 132*
  - Shaker *92*
  - Victorian 148, *148*, 151, *152, 154, 167, 168, 170, 173*, 177, *177*
- Tambour desks 72
- Tapestries 8, 9, 12, *14*, 15, 19, *99*, 100
- Tea caddies 49
- Thomire, Pierre-Philippe 129
- Tiffany, Louis Comfort *167*
- Tole ware *78, 152*
- "Trafalgar" chairs 122
- Treen 97, *127, 173*
- *Trompe l'oeil 13, 55*, 61, *162*
- Turkeywork 8, 21, 35
- Turkish carpets 35, 171
- Turner, Kenneth *107*
- Tweedy, Thomas 151

U

- Upholstery 152
- Urns *57, 101, 112, 116, 118, 121, 131, 136*

V

- Velvets 43, 46, 171
- Venetian blinds 54
- Versailles 100
- Victorian styles 144-177
- Vinyl *22, 108*, 125
- Voysey, C.F.A. 178, 180, *181*

W

- Wadsworth, Julie *180*
- Wainscot chairs 24
- Wall hangings 8, 9, 12, 15, 19, *28*, 32, 35
- Wallpapers
  - 17thC Country House 19
  - 18thC Country *74, 77, 78*
  - 19thC Classicism 104, *112*
  - American Federal 70, 71
  - Baroque/Rococo 103-104, *112*
- Wallpapers (continued)
  - Elizabethan/Jacobean 12
  - Empire 129
  - English Baroque 35
  - Georgian 46, 61
  - Regency *125*
  - Victorian *144*, 148, *151, 152, 160, 162, 168, 170, 175, 177*
- Walls
  - 17thC American Country House 24
  - 17thC Country House 19
  - 18thC Country 74, *76*
  - American Colonial 80, *80, 84, 86*, 91, *91*
  - American Empire *140*, 143
  - American Federal 70, *71*
  - Arts and Crafts 178, 180, 183
  - Baroque/Rococo *110, 112, 117*
  - Elizabethan/Jacobean 8, *9*, 17
  - Empire 118, 129
  - English Baroque 32, *34*, 37
  - Georgian 44, 46, *49*, 50, 53, 61, *69*
  - Queen Anne *39*, 43
  - Regency 118, 120, *121, 125, 129, 135*
  - Shaker *95*
  - Victorian 147, 148, *154, 160*, 170, 171, *175*, 177
- Walnut 35, 37, 43, 129, 151
- Walton, George *181*
- Warrender, Caroline *154*
- Watteau, Jean Antoine 100
- Webb, Philip 178
- Wedgewood, Josiah 54, 57
- Wells, Michael *156, 157*
- Wickham, Kate *181*
- William and Mary style 32, 37, *110, 111*
- Windows
  - 17thC Country House 21
  - 18thC Country 74
  - American Colonial 80, 91
  - American Federal 70
  - Arts and Crafts 178, 180, 183
  - Baroque/Rococo *101*, 104, 117, 119
  - Empire 129
  - English Baroque 35
  - Georgian 46, 54
  - Queen Anne 43
  - Regency 120
  - Shaker 97
  - Victorian 147, 148, *154, 160*
- Wing chairs 49, *62*
- Wyndham, Melissa *161*

Z

- Zebra wood 122

ACKNOWLEDGMENTS

In creating a book like PERIOD STYLE, so much depends on visual stimulation. If the book succeeds in stimulating, this must be due to the photographs taken by James Merrell and the art direction of Jacqui Small. Thanks are due, too, to Tommy Candler who, as always, was at hand when I was short on inspiration. And, of course, to all those whose homes are the real statement of PERIOD STYLE.

The authors and publishers would like to thank the following house-owners, interior designers, antique dealers, museums and hotels for allowing special photography for this book. The page number on which a photograph appears is followed, after an oblique or stroke, by the location on the page.

The American Museum in Britain, Claverton Manor, Bath BA2 7BD: 24, 25, 54bl, 79br, 96, 160
Cornelia Bayley, Plas Teg, Nr Mold, N. Wales: 14r, 112r, 120l, 120r, 121r, 122tr, 122bl, 122br, 123, 127tl, 161m, 164tl, 165tl
The Bell of the Bend Inn, Vicksburg, Mississippi, USA: 163bl
Cedar Grove, Vicksburg, Mississippi, USA: 153br
Rupert Cavendish Antiques, 610 Kings Road, London SW6: 2DX 118, 128
Chilston Park, Lenham, Nr Maidstone, Kent: 105bl, 106bl, 112l, 172tr, 173bl
Jane Churchill Designs Ltd, 81 Pimlico Road, London SW1 W8PH: 58, 67br, 109l, 149bl, 154lm, 162mr
The Comoglio Showroom, Paris, France: 97mr
Arnold Copper, 872 Madison Avenue, New York, NY 10021, USA: 63tr, 63br, 73l, 80, 81, 82, 83r, 86, 90, 91r, 136
Richard Davidson Antiques, Lombard Street, Petworth, W. Sussex: 18r, 21, 31l, 34tl, 106br
Hannerle Dehn, 30 Holland Park Road, London W14: 75, 100, 104bl, 105br, 116, 117
Dorney Court, Windsor, Berkshire: 14lm, 32, 41br, 161bl
Dorset Square Hotel, Dorset Square, London NW1: 67tr, 154bl
Frog Pool Farm, Avon, Somerset: 20
Geffrye Museum, Kingsland Road, London E2: lll, 11mr, 11bl, 57mt
Christophe Gollut, 116 Fulham Road, London SW3: 115r, 146, 147, 164tr, 165r
Linda Gumb, 9 Camden Passage, London N1 E2: 155, 158tl, 158bl, 159br, 162tl
Kenneth Hockin, 247 West 10th Street, New York, NY 10014, USA: 140, 141
Johnathan Hudson Interior Designs, 16 Fitzjames Avenue, London W14 ORP: 144, 145, 150
Humphrey Antiques, North Street, Petworth, W. Sussex 19r, 31l
Julian Humphreys, 25 Fournier Street, London E1: 47br, 49tl, 49bl, 49tr, 50b, 51tr
Richard Hampton Jenrette, Duchess County, New York State, USA: 71br, 130, 131, 132, 134, 135, 137, 142, 143
Erik Karlsen, Jane Churchill Ltd, Ellis House, 118-120 Garratt Lane, London SW18 4EF: 41rm, 59tr, 59tr, 66tl
Landsdowne, Natchez, Mississippi, USA: 7
Ian Lieber, Kingsmead House, 250 Kings Road, London SW3 5UH: 22, 23, 36r, 37, 102l, 149tr, 154tl
Stephen Mack Associates, Chase Hill Farm, Ashaway, Rhode Island 02804, USA 83r, 84l, 84m, 85, 87, 88, 89
The Marshalls, Brook Green, London: 5
Marshall/Shule Associates Inc., 1065 Madison Avenue, New York, NY USA: 52l, 52r, 69, 138tl
Joan Elaine Mazzola, New York and Green Farms: 73br, 105tl, 113
The Old Merchant's House, New York, USA: 153bm
Angela and Bill Page, Tunbridge Wells, Kent: 26l, 26r, 27, 28, 29, 174, 175
Parham House, Pulborough, W. Sussex: 14tl, 14bl, 16, 17, 126tl
Pavilion Designs, 49 Pavilion Road, London SW1: 153t, 171r
Saint Mary's, Bramber, Sussex 13, 15, 172tl
Dennis Severs, 18 Folgate Street, London E1: 33, 34bl, 38, 39, 40, 42, 43, 44, 45, 46, 47l, 124bl
Shaker Museum, Shaker Museum Road, Old Chatham, New York, USA: 92, 93, 94bl, 95tr, 97l, 97r
Catherine Shinn, 7 Suffolk Parade, Cheltenham, Gloucestershire: 148, 149tl, 173t
Keith Skeel Antiques, Islington High Street, London N1: 41tr, 59bl, 78tr, 106tr, 106tl, 109br, 114l, 115l, 126r, 159tr, 164tm, 164bl, 164bm, 164br, 173br
Sqerryes Court Westerham, Kent: 41tm, 59br
Henry and Irene Stewart, New York 102r, 103tr, 105tr, 105bl
Michael Strauss Ltd, 49 The Drive, Hove, Sussex: 74l, 162tr
Stuart Interiors, Barrington Court, Barrington, Ilminster, Somerset: 12, 36b, 167tr, 197br
Teneyck-Emerich Antiques, 351 Pequot Avenue, Southport, Conn., USA: 70r, 71tr, 71rm, 139r, 154tr, 107, 158r, 170
Michael Wells, Frankham, E. Sussex 98, 99, 156, 157
Garth Woodside Mansion, Hannibal, Missouri, USA: 161bl
Melissa Wyndham, 6 Sydney Street, London SW3 149br, 154br, 161tl

The following people kindly allowed us to photograph their homes:
Rosie and Michael Addison, Lee Anderson, Jane Baigent, John and Rebecca Barratt, David Cockburn and Anthony Shaw, Coline Covington, Dan and Vikki Cruickshank, Jane Cumberbach and Alistair Brown, Richard and Deirdre Davidson, Louis de Wet, John and Caroline Evetts, Ruth and Peter Fane, Piers and Caroline Feetham, Vera and Murray Gordon, Mr and Mrs Richard Gray, Deryck Healey, Charles and Maggie Jencks, Mr and Mrs Michael Keehan, Wendy Kidd, Georgia and David Langton, Ira Levy, Angela Lucas, Anna and Tony Mansi, Sue March, Christopher and Heidi Marchant-Lane, Sarah and David McElwee, Lord and Lady McAlpine of West Green, Walter and Jacqui Meyer, Freda and Jack Parker, Jo Peters, Jacinth Rhodes, mr and Mrs Espirito Santo Silva, Elspeth Riley-Smith, Dick Snyder, Anna Simonde, Mr and Mrs D. Spearing, Sarah van Gerbig, Andrew and Julie Wadsworth, Julia Walker, Michael B. White.

Music suggestions: Ambient Music Co.

Textiles by Candace Bahouth and Vanessa Robertson and furniture by Richard Latrobe Bateman, are available via the Crafts Council, 1 Oxendon Street, London SW1Y 4AT